Trade Marketing Strategies

The Marketing Series is one of the most comprehensive collections of books in marketing and sales available from the UK today.

Published by Butterworth-Heinemann on behalf of the Chartered Institute of Marketing, the series is divided into three distinct groups: *Student* (fulfilling the needs of those taking the Institute's certificate and diploma qualifications); *Professional Development* (for those on formal or self-study vocational training programmes); and *Practitioner* (presented in a more informal, motivating and highly practical manner for the busy marketer).

Formed in 1911, the Chartered Institute of Marketing is now the largest professional marketing management body in Europe with over 22,000 members and 25,000 students located worldwide. Its primary objectives are focused on the development of awareness and understanding of marketing throughout UK industry and commerce and in the raising of standards of professionalism in the education, training and practice of this key business discipline.

Books in the series

Trade Marketing Strategies

The partnership between manufacturers, brands and retailers

Second edition

Geoffrey Randall

Butterworth-Heinemann Ltd
Linacre House, Jordan Hill, Oxford OX2 8DP

A member of the Reed Elsevier plc group

OXFORD   LONDON   BOSTON
MUNICH   NEW DELHI   SINGAPORE   SYDNEY
TOKYO   TORONTO   WELLINGTON

First published as *Marketing to the Retail Trade* 1990
Reprinted 1991
Second edition 1994

British Library Cataloguing in Publication Data
Randall, Geoffrey
    Trade Marketing Strategies: The Partnership
    Between Manufacturers, Brands and
    Retailers. – 2Rev. ed. – (Marketing
    Series: Professional Development)
    I. Title II. Series
    658.8

ISBN 0 7506 2012 9

Composition by Genesis Typesetting, Rochester, Kent
Printed and bound in Great Britain by Clays, St Ives plc

Contents

Preface

This book is aimed at consumer goods manufacturers faced with the challenge of increased retailer power. The first edition assumed that, in such a fast-moving field, much of what was said then would rapidly become out of date. Indeed, many things have moved on since then, and it was considered worthwhile bringing out a revised and up-dated edition to reflect those changes. The basic message of the book, however, remains the same. It is that the power of retailers is here to stay, and that manufacturers must adapt to it. They must re-double their efforts to build and maintain strong brands, and they must radically change their strategies and structures to adapt to the new realities of dealing with retailers as partners and competitors. The situation has become more challenging, and the need to take action more urgent.

In the first edition a worst-case scenario set out what might easily be the situation in a few years' time. Summarized, it goes like this.

Social change

The trends identified accelerate. Individualism is the dominant value ('Be different from the Jones's'), leading to increasingly segmented markets . . . shoppers become increasingly demanding, sophisticated and sceptical of advertising claims and brands. Brand loyalty declines; experience of product reliability and word-of-mouth become the major influences on buying decisions.

Media effectiveness

The social changes mentioned fragment audiences: time-shifting using video-recorders and zapping of commercials means that network television cannot reach mass audiences. Cable and satellite channels fragment the audiences still further. Costs continue to rise faster than inflation.

Retailer power

Concentration continues to grow. A small number of multinational retailers emerge in each main sector; between them they account for 80 per cent of turnover. Their scanning data give them unrivalled market knowledge, which they are unwilling to share with manufacturers. Each expands its category coverage to counteract low-growth markets, so pressure on space is intensified.

Competition

With retailers dominating, the provision of adequate products produced to guaranteed quality specifications and delivered to a rigorous schedule becomes the norm. Japanese and other South-East Asian competitors enter European consumer-goods markets, applying their supreme manufacturing skills learned in other markets.

Government regulation

Governmental and supra-governmental legislation (EC) set strict controls on products, labelling and advertising, while imposing extra burdens on companies in relation to pollution, packaging and other liabilities.

Effect on manufacturers' brands

The trends produce a vicious spiral in which major brands cannot be sustained, advertising is cut, margins come under pressure, shelf space is limited, retailers' brands increase their share, new competitors are willing to meet the retailers' demands, brand loyalty is further eroded. . . .

The major manufacturers simply cannot make enough profit to reinvest in brand development and support. One by one their brands disappear from the shelves. They themselves either turn to packing for retailers, or they are taken over, or they simply die.

Note that this scenario is based on trends which already exist, and on extrapolations which are not extreme (though the conclusion may be). Everything here has been identified and commented on widely. It was a plausible hypothesis, and remains so.

The message of this book was stated then: retailer power has changed the world irrevocably, and only those manufacturers who adapt to the change will survive. Many have already started to do so; a few have gone a long way. None, in my view, has yet completed the process. That description remains essentially true. Although some firms have made major efforts to adapt, many have made only small changes, and have not yet made the radical cultural shift which is needed. There has been much talk of partnerships between manufacturers and retailers, particularly in the grocery trade, but it is to say the least unclear how much of this is talk and how much represents fundamental new ways of doing business.

Manufacturers have two – and only two – strategies for success in this new world:

- build and maintain strong brands
- deliver outstanding customer service to retailers.

The first plays to manufacturers' traditional strengths, but many firms have been neglecting the single-minded concentration on strong brands that is needed, and have been pressured into withdrawing support in the short term. This will have disastrous consequences in the medium to long term. This second edition therefore contains a new chapter wholly devoted to the issues of branding.

The second element – delivering outstanding customer service – forms the major focus of this book. To succeed, companies will need to change not only their strategies, but their culture and organization structure. The future offers the opportunity for some to gain real competitive advantage if they are radical, clear-sighted and quick enough. Those who are left behind may never catch up.

Much of the content of the book will be well known to some managers, particularly in the larger and more sophisticated manufacturing firms. Even in these, however, some parts of the book will be of interest to some people. The implications of the changes described are so profound and far-reaching, it is argued, that they go far beyond the marketing and sales functions. Chief executives, finance and production directors, indeed the board as a whole, should have faced up to the issues identified. They should at least have asked themselves certain key questions and planned actions as a result. For example:

● Has the board a genuine strategic view of its major brands, and can it commit the resources needed to maintain them against retail and competitive pressures?
● Can the board honestly say that it understands its customers in the way outlined in Chapter 3?
● Has it an information strategy which will deliver the information needed to guide corporate strategy, help decision making and control plans, as discussed in Chapter 6?
● Can the current organization design meet all the criteria laid down in Chapter 8?

Board directors in all manufacturers, then, could benefit from a selective reading of those chapters. Managers lower down who will be affected by the changes, and who perhaps are not familiar with some of the detail, will gain from a more thorough study of the whole. The book argues that from now on all functions in a firm need to be aware of customer needs, and of how their own department relates to others in delivering customer service. Accountants, computer people, production managers, those in charge of physical distribution – all are involved. They will need to work together, and will do so more effectively if they understand the whole system.

The same arguments apply, but with increased force, to medium-sized and smaller manufacturers. They are the ones who will be faced by the most severe challenges. Small local manufacturers may be able to continue to survive with niche brands and by meeting local customer needs. The forces of retailer power, technology, internationalization and new competition will hit hardest those in the middle. For them, the messages of this book are central to their survival.

The book, therefore, is aimed at practitioners – managers who have to find practical solutions to real problems. Since the field described is so fast-moving, details which will be out of date by the time of publication have been kept to a minimum. The aim is rather to identify key trends and the issues arising out of them, to assess the implications for manufacturers and to pose the crucial questions which managers must answer. Some basic description is given of such things as electronic point of sale

(EPOS), direct product profitability (DPP) and space management for the benefit of those who have not come across them. It is assumed that any one individual reading the book will already be familiar with some parts of the field: everyone should skip those parts he or she knows enough about. For this reason, anyone who does read the whole may find some repetition. Some things, such as the central importance of strong brands, are so important that it is better to repeat them too often than to risk their being missed.

A summary appears at the end of each chapter. Where appropriate, a list of further reading is given so that those who are interested may follow up some of the concepts discussed.

Although this is essentially a practical book, it will be of value to anyone studying marketing in a business school. It is my experience that most standard marketing textbooks show no awareness of the dramatic changes that have taken place in retailing and of the effects of these on the marketing job. The book will, therefore, be a valuable corrective to what seems to be an old-fashioned view presented in the existing texts.

Structure of the book

The book begins with a description of the current situation. It attempts to sort reality from some of the myths surrounding the relationship between manufacturers and retailers. It concludes that retailer power is here to stay in most markets in most countries, and that manufacturers must adapt to this fact.

Chapter 2 argues that salvation for most manufacturers lies in building and maintaining strong brands. It suggests that some companies seem to have forgotten this, and that they have lost the concentration and discipline that is needed. The advantages of successful brands, and their characteristics, are described, followed by suggestions as to the direction of future strategy. Chapter 3 argues that what manufacturers must do is apply the basic marketing principle to customers as well as to consumers – that is, they must understand them. This involves an objective and detailed understanding of who they are, what their strategies are, where your brands fit within these strategies, what their problems and opportunities are and how you can help them. As an extension, Chapter 4 looks at the particular issues raised by retailers' brands. It also raises the question of whether or not to make retailers' brands, and argues that this may be a feasible – perhaps the only – option for many manufacturers in future.

In Chapter 5 the various impacts of technology on retailers are described, since manufacturers must understand these in order to provide customer service. The newer techniques of direct product profitability and space management are discussed, together with the implications for information of EPOS and scanning.

Drawing together many of the issues from the previous three chapters, Chapter 6 discusses all the information which manufacturers need – about consumers, customers and competitors. It argues that it will be vital that a well-planned information strategy is developed to ensure that each manager has access to the right information in order to manage the customer relationship.

In Chapter 7 the difficulties of moving from the acceptance of customer needs as a driving force to a full implementation are brought out. The need to identify who in the customers' organizations you should be in contact with is described, and the need to plan and manage the relationship is argued.

Chapter 8 then goes into the details of how the company's organization structure should be adapted to cope with the new demands. It argues that in any case, the old marketing structure is no longer adequate, and the brand manager system may have outlived its usefulness. A step-by-step approach to organization design is set out, followed by a discussion of possible structures.

Chapter 9 examines how customers can be built into planning and operations by going through the elements of the marketing mix and suggesting questions to be asked and possible actions to be taken. The importance of thinking about the impact of decisions on customers at every stage is stressed.

The various aspects of increasing internationalization are discussed in Chapter 10 – consumers, retailers and manufacturers. Arguments about whether or not consumers are really becoming the same are summarized. Current developments in international links between retailers are described and reactions by manufacturers outlined. The point is made again that it is the medium-sized firms which are most vulnerable.

This leads to a look into the future in Chapter 11. A worst-case scenario is given. The implications for manufacturers are bleak. The use of alternative scenarios is recommended and the book ends with a checklist of the actions which all manufacturers should be taking in order to cope with the challenges of the future.

Geoffrey Randall

Acknowledgements

To say that many people have contributed to this book is an understatement. It would have been literally impossible without the cooperation of all those in both manufacturers and retailers who gave generously of their time, and who were generally extremely frank in discussing topics which are often sensitive. It would be invidious to single out some people as more important than others, since everyone I spoke to provided something of value. I hope that I have remembered all the names, and I trust that I have not misrepresented their views. All opinions and errors are, of course, mine.

My sincere thanks, then (in no particular order, and with the company affiliation at the time of the interview) to: Andrew Seth and Jaap Kwist, Unilever; John Millan and John Scott, Procter and Gamble; George Franzen and Herkey de Stout, Lever Brothers Company, New York; Stanley Sorkin, Supermarkets General Corporation (Pathmark); Brooke Lennon, The Grand Union Company; John Fugesi, The A and P Tea Company; Frances Cook, Nabisco Group; Andrew von Speyr, Kraft Foods; Dr John Beaumont and Ian Lemon, Institute of Grocery Distribution; Tom Vyner, I. J. Hunt and C. J. Leaver, J. Sainsbury; Jim Reed, Lever Brothers; Paul Walton, The Value Engineers; Roger Martin; Mike Clark, H. J. Heinz; Andy Thornton, Space Research International; Charles Auld; Jonathan Stowell, Van Den Bergh and Jurgens; Steve Hurst, AGB; John Fuller, Brooke Bond Oxo; Mike Butler and Ian Lane, General Foods; Richard Handover and Tom Hayhoe, W. H. Smith; David Bonner, Business Development International; Mike Thompson, Elida Gibbs; Edward Forbes, McKinsey.

May I also thank Kathryn Grant and the anonymous readers from Heinemann for helpful comments and advice. Finally, my thanks to my wife for putting up with what I take from similar acknowledgement pages to be the usual irritability of authors.

Acknowledgements to the second edition

In addition to the people whose help was acknowledged for the first edition, and whose contributions are still enshrined in the book, I should also like to thank those who gave willingly of their time in the up-dating. Again, the company affiliation at the time of the interview is given.

Mike Clark, Heinz; Andrew Seth, Lever Europe; Ric Simcock, Lever Brothers Ltd; Stephen King, WPP Group; Steve Gray, Procter and Gamble; Promotional Campaigns Ltd; Patrick Tonks, International Network Services Ltd; Chris Leaver, J. Sainsbury; D. Taylor, Safeway.

1
The problem

Everyone needs distribution

Every manufacturer needs a way of getting his or her goods to the final buyer. In some cases this may be fairly simple and direct: brewers deliver beer direct to each of their tied pubs. In other instances it may be extremely complicated: consider how many people and processes are involved in putting a can of tropical fruit on a supermarket shelf, or the personal computer I am using on to my desk.

In every case the distribution part of the process is essential and must be planned and managed. This has always been true, and marketing people have always been aware of its importance. Sometimes the distribution network has been a strategic weapon – as in Volkswagen's and the Japanese car manufacturers' attack on the US car market – and marketers have neglected it at their peril. More often, it has been taken for granted by marketing people and by top management; it is something 'out there' dealt with by the sales force and by the physical distribution department.

Recently things seem to have changed and distribution has assumed greater and greater prominence. Consider a few facts about the grocery/household product markets which can stand for a host of indicators of change:

● Twenty years ago a major UK manufacturer had almost 500 sales representatives in the field; now it has less than 100.

● In Belgium just four buying points cover about 80 per cent of Nielsen volume, while in France seven buying points have authority over some 93 per cent of packaged food distribution.

What is striking is not just that the structure of retailing has been changing – and that manufacturers have therefore had to change too – but that the resulting shift in the balance of power has produced a dramatic change in atmosphere.

The balance of power – real or phoney war?

The myth

To listen to some manufacturers you would believe that there really was a war on, and that retailers were the enemy. To be more specific, supermarket multiples are seen by some suppliers as the real competition, rather than other manufacturers.

Buyers' 'sadistic' tricks revealed

> Some professional buyers employed by large multiples are sadists who delight in humiliating their suppliers, break their promises and use a devastating weaponry of tricks and ploys to negotiate better deals. That is the view of 95 senior sales executives recently questioned. . . .Food retailers were identified as being particularly difficult to deal with. Salesmen handling these accounts showed abnormally high levels of stress. . . .The survey unwraps a Pandora's Box of alleged ploys, threats, lies and personal abuse unleashed at salesmen. . .
>
> (*The Independent*, 11 December 1987)

The Vice-President (Sales) of a major company in the USA told me that he had personally seen on a buyer's desk a list of impossible demands: 'When we have negotiated to a standstill on one, he just goes on to the next.' A very senior and respected figure in British retailing admitted that, 'Some buyers still have calluses on their knuckles where their hands drag along the ground.'

The hysteria can go higher: I have heard seasoned chief executives of major companies calling (in private) for legislation, or a cartel, to break the multiples' power.

On the other side, a senior manager of a multiple asked rhetorically, 'Who needs brands? We don't. Consumers don't. So why should they exist?'

Acceptable hyperbole, perhaps, but sophisticated senior managers from manufacturers agreed! They seemed to think it quite likely that over the next ten years or so many brands would die out, leaving only the strongest to survive.

Cooler heads on both sides reject these examples as overdramatic and unrepresentative. From a manufacturer's point of view it is vital to find out where the truth lies, for the very future of the company may depend on a correct reading of the situation and on their reaction to it.

The reality

Let us then try to look rationally at the situation. Obviously most manufacturers need distributors, and so do buyers and consumers. The very existence of intermediaries shows that they fulfil a useful economic role; all the parts of the system live together in a way biologists call symbiotic.

The nub of the problem for manufacturers is that in most markets retailers do not need all manufacturers to supply them. Since in today's crowded markets obtaining adequate distribution is a necessary condition for success, the balance of power seems to have swung towards retailers, particularly as concentration increases.

As the UK grocery market is in many ways an extreme case let us look at that first. Most people are aware from their own experience of the trend towards larger supermarkets, and of the resulting decline in the number of small independent shops. This change in structure took place rapidly from the 1950s onwards; the trend to concentration is continuing, though at a slower pace.

By 1982 the multiples had achieved a majority of grocery sales, at the expense of the cooperatives and independents of all types (only greengrocers have maintained their share, at around 4 per cent). By 1990, the top five multiples accounted for over 60 per cent of total turnover. Figure 1.1 shows the concentration curves in the UK grocery market: the top 20 per cent of stores account for fully 90 per cent of total sales.

If one looks at packaged goods – that is, the field in which most manufacturers of fast-moving consumer goods operate – the domination of the chains becomes even more apparent. In London, the largest market, just two chains – Sainsbury and Tesco – have over 50 per cent of packaged grocery sales between them.

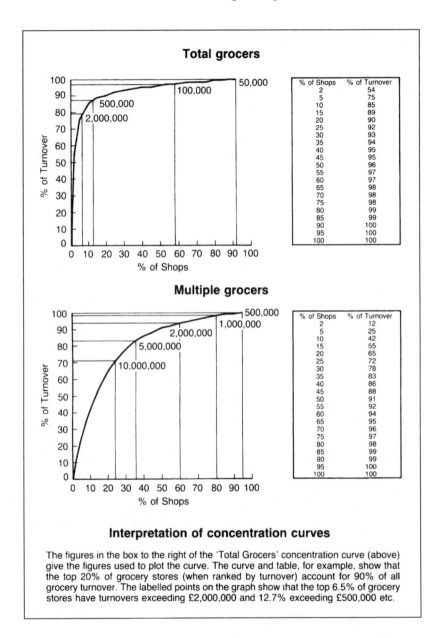

Interpretation of concentration curves

The figures in the box to the right of the 'Total Grocers' concentration curve (above) give the figures used to plot the curve. The curve and table, for example, show that the top 20% of grocery stores (when ranked by turnover) account for 90% of all grocery turnover. The labelled points on the graph show that the top 6.5% of grocery stores have turnovers exceeding £2,000,000 and 12.7% exceeding £500,000 etc.

Figure 1.1 Concentration curves in the UK grocery market, 1990. Source: Nielsen Grocery Service

There is no doubt that the multiples are continuing to strive for market share as a key to economies of scale and efficiency; the situation is dynamic, with takeovers frequent and likely to continue.

Although some retailers argue that little has changed, since some multiples (such as Sainsbury) have always had a centralized buying operation, the reality is that retail buying power is now concentrated in fewer and fewer hands. Although there is something of a cyclical pattern about the shift of responsibility, the present trend is for most major buying decisions to be centralized, and for the proportion of the market held by the top three multiples to continue growing.

Other retail sectors

If grocery is an extreme example, similar trends are at work in other markets. The market shares taken by the multiples in the different sectors vary from a fifth to over four-fifths. These figures of course hide some very large individual market shares, such as Boots, British Shoe Corporation, with over 40 per cent of footwear, and Burton with 25 per cent of the menswear market. In some sectors of its product range W. H. Smith has even higher shares.

Apart from the co-ops, which make a negligible surplus, the others show a profit margin on sales of between 2.9 per cent (Dee) and 12.8 per cent (Burton). The leaders have at times been highly rated by the Stock Exchange, which puts pressure on them to continue to perform, and punishes severely those which fall behind. This is bad for manufacturers in one sense, since retailers will pass on the pressure to their suppliers; in another sense, the increasing competition between retailers will help manufacturers.

What is certain is that retailing has become one of the most dynamic sectors of the economy. Not only in grocery, but in clothing, DIY, electrical and electronic goods, leisure services, drugstores, even books, whole new styles of operation have appeared, and corporate and individual reputations have been made (and lost). Manufacturers must come to terms with this revolution if they are to survive.

Europe, the USA and Japan

The UK – and particularly the grocery trade – has been taken as the exemplar since it is there that the transition from manufacturer domination to retailer concentration can be seen most starkly. The same trends can be seen in the rest of Europe. Indeed it could be argued that even in grocery, the leaders are chains such as Albert Heijn of the Netherlands, or Aldi or Tegelmann in Germany. The rapid development of hypermarkets in France is well known, and there is the extreme example of the Migros organization in Switzerland, which has huge shares of almost every retail market.

Overall then, the trend is to greater retail concentration and thus greater retail power. The situation in the USA is similar, though more complex. US retailers were for long regarded as the world leaders, with Sears Roebuck developing mail order last century and supermarkets appearing in America long before they came to Europe. Recently this leadership has flagged, although concepts such as direct product profitability were developed there. Certainly no one grocery multiple has the dominance of Tesco or Sainsbury, the maximum share being 4 or 5 per cent.

This national figure hides substantial regional variation, with one or two companies holding up to 50 per cent of some regions. The USA is of course a vast country, and regional variations in taste, as well as sheer transport costs, mean that all marketing is much more regionalized than we are used to (though this may be a useful model for Europe after 1992 – see Chapter 10).

The other main difference in the USA is that retailing seems much more competitive. This is a result not only of the culture, but of the sheer size of the country and of the space available. A retailer can build a large and successful business in one area, but find it difficult to extend that nationally because other chains are established in other regions. On a smaller scale, an innovative operation can be very successful, but can be copied by a competitor who builds next door. The result is that the balance of power seems much more equal between manufacturers and retailers than in Europe, although most observers think that it is moving in favour of retailers.

The USA is still a leader in innovation, and such developments as warehouse clubs and tele-shopping, discussed later, are likely to be copied elsewhere and may have a major impact on the structure of the retail trade.

The situation in Japan is notoriously different. Japan's distribution system is enormously complicated and inefficient to outsiders' eyes, and is one of the main reasons why foreigners have problems gaining entry to the Japanese market. Pressure both from other countries anxious to reduce Japan's trade imbalance and from inhabitants who discover how much more expensive goods are in Japan compared with elsewhere will change the system. The government itself is starting to take action to reduce the bad effects of sole agent agreements, secret rebates and controlled prices. The process of change may be hastened by the success of new chains such as 7–11, which has used modern methods of computerized stock control to expand rapidly to some 3500 convenience stores. This reminds us that in Western countries there are players other than the large supermarket multiples.

Convenience stores, co-ops and wholesalers

Most of the discussion so far, and indeed throughout this book, concentrates on large multiples. These are by far the most important in most markets, accounting for up to 80 per cent or so of total sales for many manufacturers. There are of course other retailers, and wholesalers, who cannot be ignored. Cash-and-carry wholesalers are important in many sectors, as are their symbol groups such as Spar in grocery or Unichem in pharmacy. Convenience stores too have made a big impact in some areas, and the cooperative chains (though still on the whole not as well managed as their major competitors) hold useful shares of some markets. New types of store also spring up, such as the convenience stores which have sprung up on petrol station forecourts in recent years. The first warehouse clubs, imported from the USA, opened in 1994. The message for manufacturers is to treat all new channels on their merits, and to try to understand their different needs. The practical problem for account managers is to persuade the company to invest in new outlets while they are still at the fledgling stage, even though such early investment may pay handsome dividends later on.

Effects on the balance of power

How can we sum up the overall effects on the relationship between retailer and supplier? Clearly one factor is going to be the relative importance of each party's business to the other.

I have previously (*Management Today*, November 1985) quoted the anonymous (perhaps apocryphal) buyer saying to the salesman, 'I account for 15 per cent of your business; you account for 5 per cent of mine. Now let's talk terms.'

Responsible retailers reject this as unacceptable behaviour. Indeed, Sainsbury's claim that the highest proportion of any major manufacturer's business that they account for is 11 per cent, the average being 3.5 per cent; the argument therefore is false, they would argue.

While accepting that, we must recognize that the sheer volume which large multiples are buying must give them a powerful bargaining tool, and that they are not slow to use it. This is what business is about, and manufacturers cannot complain about it; after all, they use the same bargaining pressure on their suppliers! Retailers also argue that since no one multiple dominates any sector, manufacturers always have a choice; if they are unhappy with the terms which one retailer insists on, they can go to all the others. This is the stuff of bargaining, and can go both ways. Let two examples suffice:

- A major petfood manufacturer was unwilling to meet the terms demanded by a multiple; the multiple then de-listed his major brands (mainly leaders in their sectors). After a few months, the manufacturer was able to demonstrate that the multiple's share of the petfood market was now several points lower than its overall market share: it was losing profit opportunities by not stocking these brands. The de-listing decision was reversed.
- Again, a multiple made demands that a manufacturer felt unable to meet (the same terms, for delivery to all 100+ stores, as had been given to two other multiples for delivery to central warehouses); although one supplier had given in, this manufacturer declined, and was de-listed. A rival retailer offered to try to make up all the lost business by giving extra display – at the expense of the supplier who had accepted the 'extortionate' demands.

These cases point to a number of issues that are central to the manufacturer–retailer relationship:

- Although retailers have bargaining power, so also do manufacturers; in particular, the traditional strength of the brand is the most valuable tool as it offers retailers the opportunity of drawing in customers not only for that brand but for all the other goods on offer.
- Rivalry between retailers is increasing; they do not act in consort, and may see competitive opportunities in difficulties a supplier is having with a rival chain.
- Negotiation is not just about whether or not to stock, and price, but includes factors such as delivery terms and service levels, credit and payment terms, parity with competitors (or exclusiveness) and so on.

In other words, we should think about the relationship not just in terms of a one-off situation. Increasingly, the trade aspect of marketing consumer products is becoming like industrial marketing: it must focus on the long-term management of a relationship which is of mutual benefit. There has been much talk of partnership between suppliers and retailers; indeed, partnership was argued in the first edition of this book to be a good model. There is room for doubt as to how real the partnership is, particularly when the balance of power is so unequal. Nevertheless, manufacturers are bound into long-term relationships with retailers, and to succeed, must manage that situation to their mutual advantage. What this means in practice is the focus of this book.

The world has changed, and will go on changing. Manufacturers must recognize this, and learn to live with it and profit from it. This book will argue that this will involve two major challenges:

● building and maintaining strong brands in increasingly hostile conditions;
● developing radically new strategies and organizational structures in order to serve retail customers supremely well.

Companies which do this will gain a real competitive advantage; those which do not will decline and die.

Summary

In most sectors, in most industrialized countries, retail concentration has increased dramatically. Buying has become more centralized, and retail management more sophisticated.

The resulting swing in the balance of power away from manufacturers and towards retailers is happening everywhere, but is most marked in the UK grocery trade. An atmosphere of hostility and suspicion grew up between some parties; saner heads see the need to work together. Partnership is discussed, but how real it is is unclear.

The details of the situation in the UK, Europe, USA and Japan vary, but the trends are similar. Manufacturers must learn to live with the new situation. Those who respond pro-actively will win, in particular by building and maintaining strong brands, and by developing radically new strategies and structures for serving retail customers.

2
Brands – the unique strategic response

The importance of brands

In responding to the new challenges posed by increasing retailer power, manufacturers have one weapon which is unique to them: strong brands which consumers want to buy and which are widely available in many different outlets. Retailers' brands, as we shall see, are a growing threat in some fields, particularly as they have improved their quality and in some cases are now seen by consumers as the equal of manufacturers' brands; but however good they are, they will be available only in one retail chain, and they are, for good and ill, indissolubly part of that chain. Manufacturers' brands can stand alone, as individuals in their own right.

There is no question that consumers want brands (despite the retailers' rhetorical question as to who needs them). The great brands are extremely long-lived. The following brands have been leaders in their category in the UK for sixty years or more:

- Hovis (wholemeal bread)
- Kellogg's (cornflakes)
- Cadbury's (chocolate)
- Gillette (razors)
- Schweppes (mixers)

- Brooke Bond (tea)
- Colgate (toothpaste)
- Kodak (photographic film)
- Hoover (vacuum cleaners).

(Murphy 1989)

Such longevity reflects not only the quality of the products themselves, but the continuing care and support lavished on their marketing by the owners (it will be interesting to see how Hoover, for example, recovers from a disastrously miscalculated promotion in 1992/93).

Some brands have established a presence globally. According to a survey in 1988 which asked consumers to rate brands by familiarity and esteem, the top world brands were:

1 Coca-Cola
2 IBM
3 Sony
4 Porsche
5 McDonalds
6 Disney
7 Honda
8 Toyota
9 Seiko
10 BMW
11 Volkswagen
12 Mercedes-Benz.

(*The Economist*, 24 Dec 1988)

World brands originate in the USA, Germany and Japan; the list is dominated by motor cars, but consumer electronics, fast food, entertainment, watches and computers are represented too. There is not a single UK entry (nor from any European country apart from Germany). In an increasingly international business world, such findings are ominous for UK manufacturers.

Longevity and world scale reflect not just skilled manufacturing or clever marketing: they reflect the fact that strong brands really are wanted by consumers. Brands play an important role in people's lives; they have their own personalities, they bring something which mere products cannot do. What exactly this is we shall explore later, but it is important to recognize and accept the fact that brands can be friends, can bring security, confidence and pleasure to people's lives. Branding is not cynical manipulation, but can genuinely contribute something which people want.

From the manufacturers' point of view, the importance of strong brands can be summed up in a few pieces of evidence brought together by Doyle (1989):

- Brands with a market share of 40 per cent generate three times the return on investment of those with a share of only 10 per cent.
- For UK grocery brands, the number one brand generates over six times the return on sales of the number two brand, while the number three and four brands are unprofitable.
- For US consumer goods, the number one brand earned a 20 per cent return, the number two earned around 5 per cent and the rest lost money.
- Small brands can be profitable: a strong brand in a niche market earns a higher return than a strong brand in a big market. In large markets, competitive threats and retailer pressure can hold back profits even for the top brand.
- Premium brands earn 20 per cent more than discount brands.
- It can cost six times as much to win new customers as to retain current users.
- The best feasible strategy to achieve profitability and growth is to focus on brand differentiation, rather than cost and price. Although the best strategy in theory is both low cost and high differentiation, in practice it is worth paying some cost penalty to achieve strong differentiation.

These are enormously powerful lessons. The basic truths behind them would be subscribed to by most marketing directors, if not by all their fellow directors on UK boards. A strong brand confers unique strengths both for defence and attack; it can outlive mere trends and fashions, and even products themselves, since the brand is stronger than the product itself. It can practically guarantee future profit streams above the norm (a fact which has been recognized in the very high multiples of earnings and assets which predators have been prepared to pay for companies such as Rowntree, Nabisco and Pillsbury which owned strong brands). In the context of this book, strong brands are the major – in some ways the only – defence against the power of retailers. You would expect, then, that companies which owned strong brands already would be going to extraordinary lengths to maintain them, and that they and others would be devoting huge efforts to building the great brands of the future. Sadly, this is so only in patches. More generally, brands are everywhere under threat.

Threats to brands

Brands are always under threat – from neglect, from competitors, from changes in the marketplace. Recently new threats have appeared, and need to be recognized and countered.

- *Fragmentation of markets*: many consumer markets are mature, and therefore at the stage when finer and finer segmentation is appearing. This is due partly to technology (in particular to flexible manufacturing techniques) and partly to manufacturers' own actions. It is also of course a response to changing economic and social trends: we now live in a period when many people want to be different from the Jones's, and have the money and time to indulge their wishes. While this offers opportunities to marketers, it is also a problem for large mass market brands.
- *Repertoire buying*: another facet of the trend mentioned above is that in some markets consumers now buy several brands for slightly different purposes; a housewife who once kept in stock only one instant coffee may now buy a cheap powder for everyday use, a more expensive type for serving to friends, a premium brand or ground for entertaining and perhaps a decaffeinated for the evenings. While it is true that in most markets consumers have always bought a repertoire of brands serially, they now stock several at the same time.
- *Media cost inflation*: in many countries the cost of heavy advertising campaigns, especially on television, has escalated far faster than most others. This has meant that it has become more and more difficult to justify the sort of spend that has traditionally been thought essential to strong brands. Again, the temptation is to look at 'cheaper' ways of achieving promotional objectives, particularly through below-the-line and cooperative advertising campaigns with retailers. This is a short-sighted view which will be returned to later.
- *Media fragmentation*: further potential problems for mass marketers are raised by the technological developments in communications – satellites, cable, pay-as-you-view, video recorders. Some commentators believe that these changes will make it increasingly difficult to reach a mass market through traditional campaigns.
- *Changing lifestyles*: the media problem is aggravated by the expanding leisure activities, and the time and money to devote to them, available to certain key target groups. They will become increasingly difficult to reach by conventional advertising.
- *Changing values*: there is anecdotal and journalistic evidence that some consumers are turning away from the glitzy, designer-everything 1980s

to a more 'authentic' search for real value for money in the 1990s – and therefore away from brands, at least if they demand too high a premium price. This may be merely a reflection of recession, and it may also be a reflection of the comparative value of manufacturers' and retailers' brands; this last point is returned to later in this chapter.

While we must recognize the reality of these external threats (and remember that some of them are opportunities too), we must also admit that the major threats to brands are self-generated. They are inter-related, and are three:

- short-termism
- greed
- neglect.

Stock markets, particularly in the USA and UK, do exert pressure on companies to keep producing earnings increases, and this does produce pressure on boards. It is still possible, however, as the lists of world and leading UK brands quoted show, to build and maintain strong brands, even with such pressures. One must suspect that some short-termism is self-inflicted, perhaps even generated by top managers' incentive reward systems. It is up to boards to develop shareholders' medium- and longer-term interests as well as quarterly earnings; sometimes, they may have to spend more time arguing a case for their long-term strategy to city analysts than they have in the past. One suspects that many do not do so now simply because they do not have a long-term strategy. It is, frankly, irresponsible of boards not to be making brand strategy one of their major priorities.

Greed is perhaps just another side of this coin. A great brand is great partly because it delivers value for money to consumers. The fact that it can earn above-average returns for its owner is tempting.

Considerable discussion was generated by the decision of Philip Morris in 1993 to reduce the price of Marlboro cigarettes (an extremely strong brand property in the recent past) by some 20 per cent in reaction to the enormous gains in market share obtained by discount brands. Why were discount brands able to gain such shares? Because the price of Marlboro had been raised by about 10 per cent a year, every year, at a time when inflation was running at around 3 per cent. In other words, Marlboro was screwing its consumers and, addicted though they are to the product, they eventually declined to go on paying the huge premium which Marlboro was asking for the value it added as a brand. Marlboro's point of difference from rivals exists, and is worth something – but there is a limit to what consumers will pay.

Neglect is perhaps a more subtle threat. Top managers have many demands on their time and energy. In recent years they have had to deal with dramatic changes in technology, sometimes volatile commodity prices, frequent turbulence in currency markets, constant pressure from competitors, increasing internationalization of their business, changes in legislation from national and supra-national bodies, and so on. They have often been pre-occupied by cost reduction, rationalization, down-sizing, international re-structuring, takeover threats. Is it asking too much of them to insist that they should still be concentrating on brand values, how to build them, how to maintain them? No, it is not. They are not paid the comparatively large sums that they receive because the job is easy. It is their duty to safeguard the future of the company as well as its present, and that future must depend crucially on strong brands. They will not be thanked for delivering results which please the stock markets this year if in the process they destroy the company potential for growth over the next ten – or fifty – years.

If these seem unduly alarmist claims, the next section will look in more detail at what has actually been happening to brands.

The effects of short-termism, greed, neglect – and retailer power

The effects of the threats outlined, and of the growth in retailer power, can be summed up in a few indicators:

- decrease in real terms in manufacturers' brand advertising and increase in retailers' spending;
- increase in the proportion of manufacturers' budgets going to sales promotion at the expense of advertising;
- decrease in consumers' perception of brand differentiation, and thus a decline in brand loyalty;
- increase in the proportion of total industry profits going to retailers at the expense of manufacturers.

These are inter-related, and will be examined in more detail.

Advertising and sales promotion

Advertising has traditionally been seen as a major part of the branding effort of manufacturers; it is the most visible part of the communication of brand values to consumers; it develops awareness, promotes reassurance, reminds buyers of the brand's qualities. While the quality of the product itself – its fitness for purpose, its ability to help consumers solve their problems – will always be paramount, advertising can add real value and personality to the brand. It is not over-stating the case to say that, at its best, advertising can enrich people's lives. Yet brand advertising by manufacturers seems to have been declining; one measure suggested that it had fallen by 64 per cent in real terms over a period when advertising by retailers increased by 40 per cent. It has also declined comparatively: while promotion to advertising ratios were about 40/60 in the USA ten years ago, they are now 60/40 and still changing.

Reasons such as media cost inflation play their part, but retailer power and short-termism are the main causes of this dramatic shift. It is much easier to give in to retailer pressure for more money by agreeing to below-the-line activity than to insist on retaining the cash to spend on advertising. This is increasingly so because better measurements show convincingly that sales promotion can have dramatic short-term effects. Well-chosen and -executed sales promotions can increase sales within a short period (say a month) by five or even ten times over normal. Such results, easily and accurately measured by current electronic point of sale (EPOS) technology, are difficult to argue against, particularly when advertising has longer-term effects which are much more difficult to measure.

However, two points may be made against this simple view, one quantitative and one qualitative. Quantitatively, it can now be shown that, although sales promotion may increase sales, it may not actually pay off in profits. Using single-source data in the USA, one major study found that only 16 per cent of promotions actually paid off when all costs and the effect of forward buying were fully taken into account. Work in the UK has also found that promotional effects are short-term.

On the other hand, similar measurements of advertising showed that, where increased advertising produced an increase in sales, this effect lasted well beyond the first year even when the heavy spending had returned to normal: the increases recorded over normal sales were 22 per cent in the first year, 17 per cent in the second and 6 per cent in the third. It is fair to record that only half the campaigns did in fact show an increase in sales for an increase in spending on advertising, but the important lesson, it is suggested, is the proof that advertising has long-term effects. Trying to justify it in months, or even a year, is misleading.

The other argument is qualitative, and concerns brand values. It is this: what does constant promotion say to the consumer about your brand? It says, I suggest, 'This brand is not really worth what we are asking you to pay for it, so here is some other inducement for you to buy'. That must be the message that consumers receive, albeit subconsciously, over periods of prolonged promotion. It is no coincidence that in product fields in which manufacturers have chosen to compete over long stretches of time by promotion and price rather than on quality and brand values, the share of retailers' brands has increased. In extreme cases such as fruit squashes, manufacturers' brands disappeared almost entirely – and it is a much more difficult and expensive business to resurrect a brand than to sustain it when it is healthy.

Decline in brand loyalty

It was suggested above that some observers feel that consumers are becoming more discerning, and that they are much less willing than they were to pay a premium for a brand. Part of this is due to manufacturers' greed, as the Marlboro example shows. Partly it is due to the excessive weight given to promotion at the expense of advertising, as was argued in the previous section. It must also be due to the greatly improved quality of retailers' brands (discussed in more detail in Chapter 4).

The evidence so far is patchy. Some is quoted by Aaker (1991).

Nielsen charted the market share for 50 selected major supermarket brands (that is, manufacturers' brands) and found that it fell 7 per cent from 1975 to 1987. The research firm NPD revealed that in a study of 20 supermarket product categories the average number of brands purchased in a six-month period increased by 9 per cent from 1975 to 1983.

The ad agency BBDO found a surprising perception of brand parity among consumers throughout the world in thirteen product categories. They asked consumers whether they felt that the brands they had to choose from in a given product category were more or less the same. Those who indicated brand parity ranged from 52 per cent for cigarettes to 76 per cent for credit cards. This was noticeably higher for such products as paper towels and dry soup, which emphasize performance benefits, than for products like cigarettes, coffee and beer, for which imagery has been the norm.

One survey of department-store shoppers involving product categories such as underwear, shoes, housewares, furniture and appliances documented the erosion of price. Only 39 per cent indicated that they paid full price, while 41 per cent waited for a sale and 16 per cent more bought discounted merchandise not on sale. *Interestingly, the study found a high negative correlation between media advertising in a product category and category sales at full price.* (My emphasis; I assume that the statement is misleadingly worded but that the conclusion is valid: the following sentence sums up that conclusion.) *Advertising, of course, creates strong brands which can hold share in the face of discounting.* (My emphasis.)

The evidence seems starkly clear: some manufacturers have not been continuing to create added value in their brands, they have been under-investing in innovation, in brand quality and in media advertising support; they have allowed retailers' brands to narrow the perceived differentiation gap. They will suffer the consequences of declining brand share, and continuing transfer of profits to retailers.

Unless, of course, they do something. There are still plenty of great brands around, and their lessons can be learned and applied.

What makes a great brand?

As I have argued elsewhere (Randall 1993 pp. 101–2), the main functions of a brand, for customers and consumers, are four.

1 *Identity:* The brand must identify itself clearly and unambiguously; name, legal protection and design elements are paramount here.
2 *Shorthand summary:* The brand identity should act as a summary of all the information held about it. Memory seems to act by storing packets of information in networks, and the brand should provide access to this network, triggering information and associations.
3 *Security:* Buying a familiar brand should be reassuring; it should guarantee to provide the benefits which are expected.
4 *Added value:* A brand must offer more than the generic product.

Although the security mentioned above is in itself of value, a brand should offer additional benefits: it should be better-quality, or better value for money, or have features and benefits not provided by the generic product. The benefits may be functional or non-functional, but they must be of value to consumers; preferably, they should be unique to the brand. What makes a successful brand can be summed up as *sustainable competitive advantage.*

Any brand which succeeds over time has something about it which is better than its competitors. The advantage must be salient to consumers or to the trade, and can flow from the product itself or from other factors. It may depend on:

- *Technology*: a technological advantage which can be protected is clearly to be desired, but is difficult to find and more difficult to protect. Threats from own label are particularly to be weighed up.
- *Production cost*: another side of technology is of course the way the product is designed and made. Marketing's role here is one of ensuring that market needs are not sacrificed to production efficiency; but a cost cushion against competitors is a tremendous asset.
- *Consumer franchise*: some brands have built up over the years a strong following amongst consumers, which is of inestimable value. Guinness, Persil and Fairy Liquid are prime examples where product quality and consistent strong marketing support over a long period have established impregnable positions. The various marques of motor car owned by the former British Leyland are counterexamples which show that consumer loyalty can be frittered away.
- *Marketing expertise*: some companies have developed great strength in one area of marketing. The Personal Care Division of the Gillette Company in the USA is very good at producing outstanding advertising; even if other elements of the marketing mix are not demonstrably better than competitors', brilliant advertising gives them an edge. Perhaps more relevant, Gillette's Shaving Products' sales force has always had a tremendous reputation in ensuring distribution and display. Note that a company does not have to be outstanding at every part of the mix: excellence in one can give a sustainable advantage, as long as it is not let down by outright failure in other areas.
- *Distribution*: of particular interest is strength in distribution. This may be gained by the range of products offered, by sales force strength, or by managing the relationship well over a period. This is the core of this book.

Strong brands which survive will be better at something important than competitors, and companies will have to be single-minded in investing management time and substantial sums of money in keeping their advantage.

The first steps – diagnosis and prognosis

The first step towards a strategy for brands must be to have a clear and objective view of where they are now. Although it would seem axiomatic that a manager should know where the profits are being made, this is surprisingly not always so. The basic information is therefore the profitability of each brand (see Chapter 6). Sales volume and value should be readily available. These should give a good picture of where we are now; but we also need to know what is likely to happen in the years to come.

Today's breadwinners: substantial volume, adequate contribution; at or near their zenith.

Tomorrow's breadwinners: show promise and reality; consumer and trade acceptance; high contribution

Productive specialities: having a limited and distinct market

Development products

Failures

Yesterday's breadwinners: still high volume, but low net revenue

Repair jobs: must have all the following:

- Substantial volume
- Considerable growth opportunities
- A significant leadership position
- High probability of exceptional results if successful
- One major defect only

Unnecessary specialities

Unjustified specialities

Investments in managerial ego

Cinderellas: sleepers who may one day awake

Figure 2.1 Drucker's categories of products

It is by looking into the future that we must supplement today's numbers. Markets are by their nature dynamic, ever-changing; the one thing we can be sure of is that the future will be different. It quickly becomes clear that trying to predict what will happen to our brands involves a host of interacting variables – economic, technological, social, competitive. Fortunately, there are some frameworks available to help cope with this complexity.

One of the original was put forward many years ago by Peter Drucker. He divided products into a number of categories (see Fig. 2.1).

Although the analysis is qualitative it has useful diagnostic value, and Drucker's insistence on the need to cut out useless products so that management energy can be focused on tomorrow's breadwinners is still valid. The scarcest resource is the time of talented management, and in British industry far too much of it has been wasted on trying to save products which were long past any useful life they may have had. Declining or small brands can of course be milked or harvested, that is, allowed to continue with minimal input of capital and management time as long as they produce profit and do not squeeze out promising new products.

There are other approaches to portfolio analysis, and what you use will depend very much on the type and size of your company and the sophistication of its planning system. All the approaches offer tools, not instant solutions; the important thing is to take a hard, objective look at your brands to see where you are now, and where you are likely to be given probable trends in the market.

Know your enemies

Part of the analysis of your brands must necessarily include a consideration of your competitors – and of possible future competitors. A senior manager of a UK multinational was shocked to find out that a Japanese company – not at that time a competitor in any of its markets – had none the less analysed the formulation of its new product in all the countries in which it had been launched. Will the Japanese be a competitor in future?

Ideally we should know as much about our competitors' brands as about our own, and ideally this information should be objective. It is interesting to see what disagreements exist between competitors as to the relative merits of brands in a market. Naturally the troops must believe in their products, but the generals – the senior management – must have objective information not only on technical performance but on buyers' views.

Further, we need to know as much as possible about our rivals' strategies, policies and tactics. Detailed knowledge of what the competition is able to do and likely to do is fundamental to out-manoeuvring them.

Since distributors are both allies and – in some markets and to some extent – competitors, we need to be very clear about their objectives and strategies. What do they really want from us? How can we help them reach their objectives while also achieving our own? How will future developments affect their attitude to our brands? This topic will be dealt with in detail in Chapter 3.

We should at this point recognize that retailers are asking the questions:

Who owns the consumer? Who does the marketing?

Branded goods manufacturers have always regarded consumers as theirs, with wholesalers and retailers as mere conduits. The whole success of a mass marketer is founded on a deep understanding of the consumer, on being able to produce what he or she wants, and on communicating the benefits to them. Retailers are now challenging that view, and arguing that the consumers are actually theirs, that they have more information about what is bought, that they are closer to the market. It follows that it is they who should do the marketing – and anyway, it is more efficient, isn't it, given the horrendous cost of television? This is a view to which manufacturers will have to have a convincing answer.

Results of diagnosis

After all this analysis, we should have a view of where our brands are now and where they are going. In relation to the trade, we may be able to categorize them in some way:

- *Strong brands*: have a sustainable competitive advantage which will ensure that the trade will want to stock them.
- *Complementary brands*: not strong in themselves, but form part of a range which consumers and the trade want.

- *Declining brands*: no sustainable advantage, vulnerable to competition or own-label; may hang on.
- *Weak brands*: me-too products with no competitive advantage; liable to de-listing.
- *Niche brands*: small share but strong loyalty from minority segment of market or trade.

Strategic choices

Unless the firm is exceptionally lucky, the diagnosis will show that some of its brands are under threat. Specifically, brands at number three or lower in the market may well lose distribution given the pressures outlined in Chapter 1. Some firms may find at this stage that they have no strong brand which is likely to survive. It is difficult to overemphasize this point, which many manufacturers seem not yet to have grasped.

Many or most brands which are not number one or two, or do not have strong niche benefits, will be de-listed and will not survive in the major multiples (which will account for the lion's share of most markets). This is a strong statement, but one which I believe is amply supported by trends currently visible in the marketplace.

What are the strategic choices?

First, assuming that you wish to stay in branded goods, one or more brands must be identified which will be maintained as – or made into – strong survivors. These should be brand leader or number two, or realistically capable of reaching that level.

Second, brands lower than number two must be examined objectively to see if they can be sustained as, or made into, niche brands. Plenty of such brands exist, but finding profitable niches which can be defended is not easy – and all your competitors will be trying to do it too!

Third, a serious new brand development policy should be drawn up. This is a huge topic on its own. In this context let us just say that the influence of the trade should be borne in mind, not necessarily as an overriding factor, but as an important one. They should be involved as early as possible.

Fourth, decisions must be made about those brands identified as vulnerable. Sentiment must be put aside and objective conclusions reached. Drucker argues that one serious attempt only should be made to rescue a weak brand: after that, it should be killed. For most weak brands death is the only solution, though milking for profit may be arguable for a time as long as this does not divert managerial or other resources from more important products.

Finally, the firm must decide what its future position will be on making own-label products. Even companies which pack for retailers now should, I suggest, review this decision. It is a difficult and complicated one, and will be treated in Chapter 4.

Building and maintaining brands

The critical success factors in building and maintaining a brand have been discussed, either explicitly or implicitly, in what has gone before. They have not always been evident in what companies are actually doing, but they are essential for future success. They are: quality, differentiation, consistency, evolution and support.

Quality is fundamental, and must remain at the forefront of everyone's mind. Two familiar points must be reiterated: quality must be defined from the consumer's point of view, and it is the quality of the total offering that is important. While the quality must be seen from the consumer's point of view, it is the manufacturer's skill and commitment which will continue to deliver it. The quality is what the target segment wants, so McDonald's is outstanding at delivering quality to its consumers even though middle-class critics may sneer at its products. What IBM has delivered over the years when it has led the world computer market is the quality of its hardware, software and service support; the fact that it has not necessarily been at the leading edge of technology has been less important. Recently, it has spectacularly failed to keep up with very rapidly changing market demand.

Differentiation is self-explanatory but difficult to achieve. Whether expressed in the old phrase of a unique selling proposition (USP), or in the more modern terminology of sustainable competitive advantage, the brand must have something which differentiates it from its competitors. Moreover, the something must be salient to the target consumers, that is, it must motivate them to buy; even if the difference is small, it must be relevant. It may be intangible, as in the quality of service or the psychological benefits delivered, but it must be perceptible. It can be pre-emptive, in the sense that other products have the characteristic but the first one to claim it keeps it. While such differentiation by small, psychological differences does work sometimes, however, the goal for all manufacturers should be real functional difference, based on sedulous, long-term research and development. Such functional differences will provide the platform which will be most difficult to copy, both by competitors and by the retailers.

Consistency is a hallmark of great brands. Chopping and changing from year to year (or brand manager to brand manager) may be exciting, but it risks confusing and alienating consumers. The value of a successful brand is so great that a sensible company makes changes only after the most thorough consideration. This does not mean that no change is desirable – quite the contrary.

Evolution is essential, since the environment and the market are always changing. Fairy Liquid remained the leading washing-up liquid in the UK for many years on a platform of softness and kindness to the hands. Without abandoning that claim, it then moved on to a longer-lasting, value-for-money position; it has now been re-launched on a grease-dissolving differentiation. All relate to overall product quality. Other great brands such as Persil or Guinness have been famous for the consistency of their branding, although the actual campaigns have changed substantially over the years in response to changing social and market influences.

Support may mean different things in different contexts, but always involves substantial investment. For fast-moving consumer goods, as has been extensively argued above, it usually means heavy expenditure on above-the-line advertising to maintain awareness and reinforce brand values; not even the strongest brand can rely on its past reputation for long. For industrial brands, it may involve serious commitment to after-sales service, or high research and development costs. For service companies, the need may be for very large expenditure on staff training. An unfortunate effect of identifying some brands as Cash Cows (in the terminology of the Boston Consulting Group) is that top management tries to siphon off funds from successful brands to invest elsewhere, not realizing that a leading brand will not stay in that position without continuing substantial support. Any signs of this tendency must be resisted, though scarce resources often make the dilemma acute.

Finally, it is worth summarizing the view of Stephen King, that we are now moving into a different world, in which not only is the majority of an industrialized economy made up of service businesses rather than manufactured products, but that all products contain a large service element. In this new world, the old recipes may not be adequate. King suggests (King 1991) that consumers are different in that they are much less ready to accept authority figures, including the brand as authority;

that most service-based products can readily be copied; that the points of contact for a company brand are more diverse than for a product-based brand (a point which will in fact be taken up later in this book); and that discriminators are based on people, not things. King suggests that new elements of strategy will therefore become more important, in particular the staff as brand-builders and the organization structure, in addition to the more traditional, but in future more difficult, areas of the brand idea and the communication of brand values. Much of the rest of this book will in fact illustrate and support those views.

Summary

All firms must fight for survival and profit. For manufacturers of consumer goods this must mean strong brands.

Great brands are extremely long-lived. They are also more profitable than lesser brands, and offer manufacturers the main – perhaps only – hope in resisting retailer power.

But, along with external threats to brands, there are serious internal threats caused by:

- short-termism
- greed
- neglect

Companies have reduced real spending on advertising for brands, and increased sales promotion. Although promotion can have dramatic short-term effects, its longer-term results may be disastrous. Brands risk losing consumers' confidence and trust. The main functions of a brand are:

- identity
- shorthand summary
- security
- added value

A brand's sustainable competitive advantage may come from:

- technology
- production costs
- consumer franchise
- marketing expertise
- distribution

Firms must start with an objective diagnosis of where their brands are now, and a look into the future to see where they may be going.

They should categorise the brands in terms of whether they will be:

- strong brands
- complementary brands
- declining brands
- weak brands
- niche brands

Brands holding less than number two position in their category will be de-listed unless they have sustainable niche strengths. Key to building and maintaining strong brands are:

- quality
- differentiation
- consistency
- evolution
- support

Findings on brand profitability point to the value of being market leader; brands below number two are unlikely to be profitable. But small brands can be profitable if they are strong in a niche; a strong niche brand may be more profitable than a strong brand in a large market.

Competitor intelligence is a vital input to strategic decisions: it is important to know your enemies. A consideration of competitors should include potential new entrants, and customers.

Further reading

Aaker, David A. (1991) *Managing Brand Equity*, New York: The Free Press

de Chernatony, L. and McDonald, M. (1992) *Creating powerful brands*, Oxford: Butterworth-Heinemann

Doyle, Peter (1989) The strategic options. In: *The Brand is the Business: The Strategic Importance of Brands*, London: The Economist Conference Unit

Drucker, Peter F. (1967) *Managing for Results*, Oxford: Heinemann

King, S. (1991) Brand-building in the 1990s. *Journal of Marketing Management*, 7, 3–13

Macrae, Chris (1991) *World Class Brands*, Wokingham: Addison Wesley

Murphy, J. (1989) *Brand Valuation*, London: Hutchinson

Randall, G. (1993) *Principles of Marketing*, London: Routledge

For concepts such as portfolio analysis techniques, see any major marketing management text. A useful summary is the chapter 'Analytical frameworks for strategic market planning' in Baker, Michael J. *et al.* (1983), *Marketing: Theory and Practice*, 2nd edn, London: Macmillan

3
Understanding your customers

The underlying theme of this book is simple: the basic principles of marketing should be applied to retailers as customers. Put like that, it looks oversimple, a truism. My belief is that marketing is indeed simple, as an overriding business idea. The problem is that most people do not put it into practice, partly of course because it is in fact extremely difficult. What so often distinguishes successful firms from their less successful competitors is that the good firms actually do what they say they do. If they say they are committed to new product development they actually do put top management time and support, and the necessary funding, behind new ideas and brands. If they say that they are committed to quality then they put huge efforts into translating that into effective action throughout the company's operations. If they say that they are sensitive to customers' needs then they try hard to find out what those needs are, and make genuine efforts to meet them. Putting these simple ideas into practice – every day, every week, every month – takes determination as well as clear-sightedness, the will to question every established practice and the flexibility to change what is no longer appropriate. There are also enormous internal political problems involved in changing an established structure or way of doing things.

Let us then return to what I take to be the first and most basic marketing principle: understand your customer.

We have already noted that the wellspring of this book is the dramatic change in the balance of power between manufacturers and retailers. We have noted too that this has resulted in feelings amongst some manufacturers which are hysterical if not downright paranoid. This attitude towards retailers – 'They're the enemy...they're just parasites...they're destroying our markets...' – must be set aside. Understanding demands empathy – the ability to put yourself in the other person's shoes and feel what they feel. If we are to work with retailers, and we must, then we need to see where they are coming from and, more importantly, where they are trying to go. We need to ask: what are their goals and strategies? What problems do they have in achieving their objectives? Where do our products fit into their overall operation? How can what we do be adjusted so that it helps rather than hinders them?

Let us summarize first the main trends in retailing which may affect our relationship with our customers. The issue of power has been covered, and can be summarized as: in virtually all markets, in most countries, the trend is towards greater concentration in retailing, and therefore the balance of power is swinging towards retailers.

One of the effects of this is that the buying operation has become much more sophisticated. Retailing as a career used not to attract a very high calibre of entrant, but this has changed. Major retailers now recruit large numbers of graduates and educated 18-year-olds, and have high-quality training programmes. The calibre of managers, and the rewards they can earn, are very much higher than a few years ago. The intellectual and managerial quality of the management team in a major retailer is now at least the equal of that in a manufacturer. This trend towards more sophisticated managers is seen right down through the organization.

Allied to this is the tendency towards centralization of buying decisions. More sophisticated management and better information systems mean that most retailers feel that all major buying decisions can be better made at Head Office than by every branch manager separately. The extent to which this applies obviously varies; in the USA many decisions are still made locally or at least regionally; some multiples are very much less centralized than the most extreme examples; some chains are beginning to experiment with going back to allowing the local manager some freedom (in France, some local supermarket managers have discretion in buying local fresh produce and cheeses). Overall, though, the trend is clearly towards the centre and therefore fewer buying points.

The information revolution, too, is in itself a major change. The amount and quality of information available to retailers through electronic systems is now huge, and gives them enormous potential advantages. This theme will be returned to in more detail later.

The last three trends together mean that at the sophisticated centre there are probably more buyers per product field than previously. Many retailers now have buying teams with marketing and merchandising representatives, for example. Within a product field there will be more specialist buyers, each concentrating on a narrow category. As we shall see in Chapter 6, new relationships mean that manufacturers need to call on more functions and more people in retailers than just buyers.

At a broader level, there are several trends which are affecting retailers; some are contradictory, and their overall effect is not always easy to gauge. For example, there is both a trend towards wider range and towards greater specialization. Many multiples, finding growth difficult to sustain in their core business, are moving into new merchandise areas. Many – Boots, W. H. Smith, Sainsbury – have moved from different fields into DIY; fashion retailers have expanded into children's wear and furniture; and so on. Sometimes the expansion is for a very specific purpose. In the USA the extremely successful Toys'R'Us chain found that their further growth was limited by the low number of visits per year made by the average customer: they introduced disposable nappies sold at cost or as a loss leader, and doubled the number of visits (and incidentally became the biggest retailer of disposable nappies in the country).

Contrary examples are the successful new chains specializing in a very narrow field: Tie Rack, Sock Shop and their imitators; the croissant and cookie chains, etc.

A reflection of the increasing sophistication of retail management has been the tendency to segment markets and target chains at specific age and lifestyle groups. The honour of starting this is generally given to George Davies of Next, but the lessons have been applied by others such as Burton's. The latter has also begun to adjust the chain's positioning (and therefore product range) to the changing demographic structure of the population. The spectacular successes and equally spectacular failures of retail multiples remind us that this process of adapting to changing consumer tastes is a constant challenge; getting it right this year does not guarantee success in five years' time.

There are of course also threats to retailers, other problems with which they have to cope. It is important to understand these as part of the process of standing in their shoes.

Competition

There is a high degree of rivalry both within and between sectors. As in any successful business, innovations are rapidly copied if possible.

Compared with manufactured goods, new retailing ideas can rarely be protected by patent or copyright; only the continuing flair and skill of the retailer can guarantee future growth. In what is now a high-visibility sector, current and potential rivals are on the look-out for growing markets and successful innovations. This scanning now takes place on an international scale; ideas on the future of retailing are now sought not just in the traditional North American markets but also in South-East Asia, particularly in Japan. Although in many markets there is still a little natural growth left for the expanding multiple, in many the scope for gaining further share from old and inefficient independents and co-ops is limited.

There are also new competitors entering some markets. Warehouse clubs have expanded rapidly across the USA from their original base in California, and look set to spread in Europe; a legal challenge by the three top supermarket multiples in the UK in 1993 failed to stop planning permission for Costco to open a warehouse club in Essex. These clubs can offer very significant savings to consumers (25 to 40 per cent off normal retail prices) and seem certain to take business away from current retailers (though perhaps more from mail order, department stores and other consumer-durable retailers than from supermarkets). Convenience stores on petrol stations are also growing in number; they may be relatively small at the moment, and perhaps more of a threat to other convenience stores than to full-line high street shops, but they are symptomatic of the dynamic nature of the market. No retailer can afford to be complacent.

New competitors are also increasingly coming from abroad. Chapter 10 deals with this topic in more detail, but we may note here that successful entrants to the UK range from well-established chains such as Benetton to newer ones such as IKEA in furniture/household products to grocery discounters Aldi and Netto.

Stock market pressure

Because of their very success, many retailers became stock market darlings, with high price/earnings ratios and equity prices. As business people who have enjoyed similar status will recognize, such adulation is all too short-lived. Expectations grow with the price, and any shortfall from these exaggerated hopes is punished by the market. Because of the prevalence of hostile takeover bids, both within countries and increasingly internationally, a weak share price makes a company feel very vulnerable (and correspondingly, a strong share price offers opportunities for growth by acquisition). Boards of directors, therefore, constantly seek to continue to show growth in sales, profitability and return on capital. This inevitably feeds through to pressure on buyers not only to stock goods which will sell (which after all is in the interest of both retailers and manufacturers), but also to squeeze extra margin out of the manufacturer. This, and the increasing competition mentioned, leads retailers such as Sainsbury to say publicly that suppliers will be expected to share in the pain of the low price tactics they are forced to adopt.

Demands on capital and cash

The growth of retailers has so far been based to a large extent on either the acquisition of new sites, or the redevelopment of existing ones, or both. These are extremely expensive, with the cost of a new store running into many millions of pounds. In some countries, such as the USA, land is relatively freely available, whereas in many European countries or Japan the limited amount of land means that prices have become prohibitive. Allied to the competition and pressure for growth, this means that some retailers are having to fund huge development programmes. If land is freely available, then competition means that it is likely that promising areas will become 'overshopped'. If land is scarce, the successful bidder has a huge investment to recover and make profitable.

Moreover, the very sensitivity to market trends which has brought success to retailers has meant that for some the life cycle of a particular 'product' – positioning, target market, design, shop-fitting, layout, merchandise range – has become shorter and shorter. Some chains now expect to have to redesign their stores completely every eighteen months to three years.

Another demand on cash is the need for new technology: although electronic point of sale (EPOS) and scanning equipment offer tremendous benefits to retailers, they are not free. They also need support from expensive and highly trained staff. (The whole area of information technology and its impact on retailers is dealt with in more detail in Chapter 4.)

This leads on to the other area of increasing pressure on costs for retailers – staff. In many countries the early to mid-1990s will see a drastic reduction in the size of the 18–24-year-old population (25 to 33 per cent in some cases). It appeared at one time that many companies, both manufacturers and retailers, would be fighting to attract and retain these people. Retailers are perhaps in a more difficult position in that they have come later to the field of recruiting and developing highly qualified staff than many manufacturers. The recessionary climate of the late 80s and early 90s has partly dissipated this fear, and many groups were looking to replace full-time staff with many more part-timers. It is not yet clear how successful this strategy will be, given the increasing demands for quality of service. The demands of running a high-quality service operation also place a premium on training; increasing sophistication in technology and methods only adds to this cost element.

Changing consumer habits and expectations

In many countries there is evidence of a decline in the number of shopping trips. This results from a number of socioeconomic trends – increasing numbers of working wives/mothers, changing gender roles, increasing car ownership, wider variety of leisure activities – which are altering the place of shopping in many people's lives. The effect on retailers is that they have to make the most of the time that their consumers spend in the store, as a lost opportunity will not be made up so easily. Consumers are also becoming more demanding in what they expect from shopping (as from other parts of their lives). Increasingly they are looking for an experience which gives rewards other than the merely functional. This puts pressure on the retailers to anticipate and respond to changing tastes and expectations (with corresponding cost implications).

A further complication is the development of new shopping methods, in particular those growing from new technology. Some commentators predict an important role for 'armchair shopping' in which the consumer uses a home computer terminal (or pad connected to the television) to scan product offerings, select purchases, and pay. In the USA now, whole cable TV channels are devoted to home shopping, and the top two companies in the field, QVC (standing for Quality, Value and Convenience) and Home Shopping Network (HSN), had combined revenues in 1992 of $1.5 billion (a 76 per cent increase from 1989); they have subsequently talked about merging to form a serious new challenge to existing shops (though at the time of writing the merger had been – perhaps temporarily – called off). HSN reaches some 60 million households, so home shopping is no longer confined to a tiny minority. The audience reached is not very different from the general population.

At this stage it is difficult to predict how far such methods will penetrate: it seems certain that some market share will be achieved.

Obviously the trend must be watched carefully, particularly for specific segments such as highly educated, high-earning families who may be most attracted to the new channel and who are anyway difficult to reach. It is possible that the main retail competitors to be affected will be catalogue distributors, so suppliers who have large businesses through that channel will need to be particularly vigilant.

Home shopping is now being launched in the UK. One school of thought holds that this development may give some power back to manufacturers if it really takes off.

Squeeze on space

The growing number of products stocked by many retailers results both from their own desire to grow and from manufacturers' wish to produce growing sales and profits. Although some retailers have drawn back from haphazard expansion into new product sectors and are concentrating on their core businesses (e.g. W. H. Smith in the UK), the overall trend is towards more categories, brands, varieties, sizes. As there appears to be a limit to the economies of scale offered by ever-larger stores, the inevitable result is pressure on the available shelf space. The growth of retailers' brands aggravates the situation. Use of more sophisticated techniques can help retailers to evaluate the contribution of individual products more accurately than before, but in the end it is their flair and judgement as to what range will maximize customer appeal and profit which will determine which products are stocked and which are de-listed. This is a particularly sensitive topic for manufacturers, and one to which they themselves contribute, for example by range and variety extension. It will necessarily be returned to later.

Political intervention

Where a few companies dominate any industry, there will be some people worried about the effects of possible monopoly/oligopoly power. This is true of retailer power, although the criticisms so far have been muted as the retailers have been able to convince the politicians and regulators that their efficiencies are delivering benefits to consumers. There are, however, growing complaints:

- that these benefits are illusory and that prices are higher than they need be;
- that the profit levels of some retailers, especially UK grocery multiples, are significantly higher than those in other countries (up to 8 per cent margin on sales compared with around 2 per cent elsewhere);
- that the social effect of retail multiples on town centres and local shops is disastrous;
- and, potentially most damaging, that because of the move to very large out-of-town stores, the worst-off members of society are badly served by the multiples, and end up paying higher prices for worse-quality products (especially food) than their better-off fellow-citizens.

Retailers have answers to many of these criticisms, but the chorus of complaint is growing louder. France has recently called a halt to unbridled expansion of out-of-town superstores, and many in the UK would like to see a similar policy. This is unlikely at present, but social and political resistance may limit the retailers' ambitions in the end.

To summarize, there are numerous trends and pressures affecting retailers: manufacturers must understand these if they are to be able to talk sensibly to their customers. It may not solve the national account negotiator's problem when faced with a seemingly outrageous demand on a Friday afternoon to understand that the buyer is also under extreme pressure to perform; but that understanding should inform the manufacturer's planning and management of the relationship with the retailer all the time.

Beyond generalities, of course, the manufacturer must study and understand each customer as an individual firm. This necessarily means a general understanding of the structure of that market and the forces which are driving its development. The individual manufacturer needs to look beyond each customer to its markets – almost certainly wider than the manufacturer's own (at least than those of the business unit which is carrying out the analysis). Then the particular situation of each retailer must be examined in detail.

As a minimum, the following questions must be asked:

- What are the major trends affecting buying patterns in the retailer's markets – social, attitudinal, demographic, economic?
- What major forces from outside the current structure might affect the retailer's business in the next few years? These might include technological changes such as tele-shopping, political/legal changes such as Sunday opening, or demographic changes affecting staffing.

- What changes in the overall pattern of distribution channels may affect the retailer's business? This will include changes in transport systems and costs, encroachment from other retail sectors, new forms of competition (such as warehouse clubs).
- What is the current competitive structure of the retailer's sector and what trends are visible? Relevant here are current market shares and trends, likely developments (in, for example, discounting, specialization such as Sock Shop) and strategic groups (the reader is referred to the work of Michael Porter for further detail on these concepts).
- What is the current competitive position of this firm? Market share, sales volume and value, profitability, share price are likely to be of interest. Customer and expert views of the firm's image would also be valuable.
- What is the company strategy – what are its chosen target markets and segments, what is its overall positioning, how does it try to achieve its objectives in terms of operating policies? A standard SWOT analysis (strengths, weaknesses, opportunities, threats) is appropriate as a framework against which to try to understand what the firm is attempting to achieve.
- Specifically, how does the retailer's merchandising policy (that is, its decisions of what products to stock and how to display and promote them) fit within its overall strategy? What precisely is it trying to achieve with its product range: is it trying to move up market, or to present a value-for-money image; to offer depth within a fairly narrow range or to provide relatively shallow coverage of a very wide product mix; to target a very precisely defined market segment or to appeal to the broad middle market?
- What is its policy on retailers' own brands and how does this relate to its overall position and strategy? This topic is returned to in Chapter 4.
- Within your own product fields, how do your products and brands relate to the broader strategies identified? How can your brands help the retailer to achieve his or her objectives? Are your product fields essential to the retailer in that they form a major reason for consumers to go to that store, or peripheral? Is each of your product fields more profitable to the retailer than some others, average, or less profitable?
- More specifically, how do your products shape up in terms of direct product profitability? Are they easy to handle and display, or difficult? Do they take up a large amount of space in relation to their sales or a little? (The topics of direct product profitability (DPP) and space management are covered in Chapter 5.)

- What are the retailers' physical distribution policies and, more important, what are their aspirations? How does physical distribution fit within their strategy, is it a major factor in a cost-cutting programme? Are they moving to central warehousing, or direct store delivery, and why? How are goods actually handled between depots and stores, and within warehouses and stores?
- How is technology changing the business? EPOS and scanning are obvious influences, but more important is how the retailer is going to use the data flowing from the new systems: how will they affect his or her view of the business, and in particular of your products' contribution to that business? Will technology have a more profound impact on the whole business (see Chapter 5)?
- Who are the people running the business, at all levels? What sort of people are they, what are their aspirations, what are they trying to achieve, what are their difficulties and problems? What is the company culture – relaxed and friendly, or formal; inflexible and rule-bound, or flexible and open to individual initiative?
- Who really makes what decisions, who influences them, who controls the flow of information, how are decisions made, which policies are set in concrete and which can be bent a little?

It is perhaps worth stressing that the approach advocated here has been routinely used for many years by companies in the field of industrial marketing – that is, firms selling to other manufacturers – but is less common amongst consumer goods manufacturers. Once an industrial goods manufacturer has adopted the marketing approach (beautifully summed up by the Chairman of the Carborundum Corporation, who used to make grinding wheels, as, 'Our customers don't want grinding wheels, they want metal removed'), they know that they have to understand their customers' businesses very well, and that they have to identify all the buying influences affecting the purchase of their products. The identification of the so-called decision making unit is central to industrial marketing, and the model is a useful one for consumer manufacturers to study. Depending on the nature of the buying decision (major or minor, new purchase, modified rebuy or standard rebuy and so on), different people will have different roles and influences on the purchase decision. The marketer needs to identify these so that appropriate strategies and tactics can be brought to bear – sometimes over a long period – on all those involved. The analogy with selling to retailers will be clear.

In case readers think that too much is being made of this issue, one eye-opening example will be quoted: a major manufacturer carried out a detailed study of one of its retail customers – it identified no less than fifty people with whom they ought to be in contact. Not all these needed to be seen every week, and not all would be visited by the sales or even marketing staff. All, however, had a potential impact on the relationship between the two parties; the manufacturer needed to take the reaction of each into account in relation to some aspect of the business, and might have wanted to influence each at some time. How many people have you identified in each of your major customers?

It has seemed for some time that the supposed divide between industrial and consumer marketing was more apparent than real, and I have argued that there is in fact a convergence between the two. While industrial manufacturers are learning from consumer-goods marketers about branding, the latter can learn a lot from their industrial colleagues about managing a relationship over time. To ask, 'How can I help this retailer do his or her job better?' may seem a drastic attitudinal change for the typical manufacturer, but that is the goal to aim for.

All this attitudinal change and deep study of retailers is of course not just for fun: we should never lose sight of the fact that the overriding purpose is to increase the profitability of the manufacturer. By understanding and meeting the retailer's needs better than competitors, the manufacturer will improve his or her relative position, support existing brands and be better placed to introduce successful new ones.

Summary

Manufacturers must learn to apply the basic principles of marketing to retailers as well as to consumers. This means empathy not hysteria.

The main trends which are affecting retailers are:

- Higher quality management.
- More centralized buying.
- More and better information.
- More buying groups and more people per group.
- Difficulties in sustaining growth rates.
- Lifestyle segmentation.

There are also major threats to be dealt with:

- Increasing rivalry.
- Ease of copying successful formats.

- Stock market pressure.
- Demands on cash for development, from shorter life cycles, new technology and scarcer staff.
- Changing consumer expectations.
- New forms of shopping.
- Squeeze on space from extra categories.
- Social and political resistance to the effects of retail power.

To understand individual customers, manufacturers must be able to answer a series of questions about them:

- What major forces outside retailing will affect their business?
- What changes in the overall patterns of distribution will affect them?
- What is the current competitive structure of the sector?
- What is the competitive position of this company?
- What is its corporate strategy in terms of target markets and segments, positioning; what are its strengths, weaknesses, opportunities, threats?
- How does its merchandising fit within this strategy?
- What is its policy on retailers' brands?
- How do your brands fit within these policies?
- Specifically, what is your DPP position?
- What is their physical distribution strategy?
- How is new technology affecting them?
- Who are the people running the business?
- Who makes what decisions?

Manufacturers who truly understand their customers and are proactive in trying to meet their needs will have a competitive advantage.

Further reading

Porter, M. (1980), *Competitive Strategy*, New York: The Free Press
Porter, M. (1985), *Competitive Advantage*, New York: The Free Press
Porter, M. (1980), *The Competitive Advantage of Nations*, New York: The Free Press

4
Retailers' brands

Retailers' brands – or own brand, own label, private label, private brand, distributors' own brand, retailer-originated brand – are at the heart of the new relationship between manufacturers and retailers. In a sense they represent a return to retailers' traditional role: manufacturers' brands are after all hardly a century old. For most people, though, retailers' brands are a recent phenomenon; if the 1960s were the high point of manufacturers' brands, the 1980s saw the flowering of retailers' brands in many fields.

Some own-label shares of grocery markets are shown in Figure 4.1. They range from under 10 per cent to over 60 per cent, with an overall share of 24 per cent. In health and beauty markets, own-label shares range from under 10 per cent (toothpastes, deodorants and body sprays, razors and blades, tampons) to 25 per cent (hair gels). In the light of previous and subsequent discussion of strong branding, the differing levels of own-label penetration are interesting.

Certainly own label is a bone of contention between the parties. Manufacturers claim that they spend all the development time and money to produce a new brand only to find that retailers, having waited long enough to see if it will survive, merely copy it and sell the copy at a lower price. Some go further and claim not only that own-label products are parasitic on manufacturers' brands, but that they depress markets by concentrating on low price, thereby devaluing the product in consumers' eyes. If manufacturers cannot rely on recouping the huge development outlays by selling at a reasonable price protected from own label, they will cease to innovate and everyone – not least consumers – will suffer.

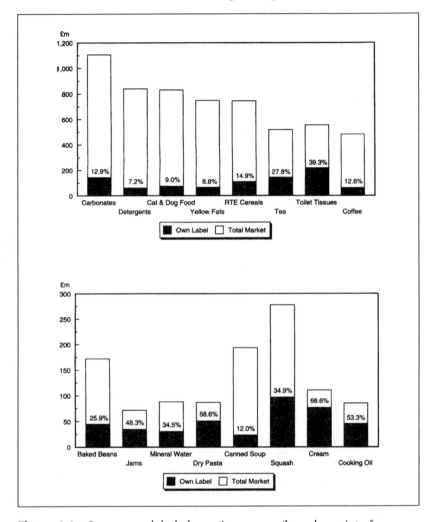

Figure 4.1 Some own-label shares in grocers (based on sixty-four product categories, year ending December 1992), Source: Nielsen Grocery Service

Retailers retaliate by saying that manufacturers are not very good at new brand development anyway: most launches fail, and do so because they are me-too's with no real consumer advantage. The torch of innovation has passed to retailers, they claim, as they are now closer to the market and more sensitive to consumers' needs.

There is, of course, much to be said on both sides. The whole issue is of central importance and worth dwelling on, as it raises very fundamental questions about marketing:

● Who owns the consumer? Who knows most about her or him?
● Who owns the store? Is the retailer controlling the market, or just a property owner renting out space?
● Who should be doing the marketing job, from innovation through product policy to advertising and promotion?
● Who needs brands, apart from the manufacturers?
● What actually is a brand anyway?

These questions have come to the fore because of the dramatic rise of retailer concentration, and the consequent increase in retailers' brands as a proportion of many markets; this has been reinforced by the changing role of retailers' brands from merely being cheap copies to achieving parity of quality with manufacturer' brands in some fields. Let us first clarify what is meant by retailers' brands, at the same time looking at some of their manifestations.

Own-label brands, as they used commonly to be called, came to prominence in supermarkets at a particular time and reflecting the grocers' particular needs. The supermarket chains were competing mainly on price, and own labels were used as part of this strategy. They were usually a slightly inferior version of the leading brand, sold at a lower price, with packaging reflecting this positioning. This view is now out of date. Many retailers' brands are – and more importantly are seen by consumers as - equal or superior to manufacturers' brands. Marks and Spencer's St Michael brand is enormously powerful, and so now is Sainsbury's; Boots' brand name in some fields is very strong, and there are similar examples in other fields. In some markets, the research and development carried out by retailers is greater than that of manufacturers, and the design and presentation of brands is superior. In some research by Cambridge Consultants, seven of the top ten new products as rated by consumers were retailers' brands.

Thus, we must look at retailers' brands as genuine brands in their own right, as well as just imitations; and we need to distinguish between different types of retailers' brands.

Figure 4.2 summarizes the different types of retailers' brands; a fuller description is given in Appendix 1.

There are of course variations on these basic types, for example, although Sainsbury mainly uses its store name for its own brands, it has

Store name brands: most grocery brands fall into this category. Examples are Sainsbury in the UK, Kroger in the USA, Aldi in Germany and Albert Heijn in Holland

Retailer-controlled name brands: the best-known example is of course Marks and Spencer's St Michael name, which is more or less synonymous with its owner. The case of Sainsbury's Novon is discussed below

Designer labels: these are not confined to manufacturers, but have been adopted by some retailers as well

Licensed names: a similar tactic is the identification of a range with a famous personality (real or imaginary), but exclusive to one retailer

Generics: these are absolutely basic products, usually limited to a few commodity fields such as sugar, packaged in very plain style and sold at a rock-bottom price

Figure 4.2   Retailers' brands

also launched products bearing a specific brand name – Vitapint for its enriched skimmed milk and Supreme for a pet food.

The development which sent shock waves through the industry was the launch in the autumn of 1992 of Sainsbury's Novon range of laundry detergents. It had traditionally been thought that retailers' brands were aimed mainly at the soft underbelly of manufacturers' brands, that is those where quality and differentiation were weak, and little support was provided; markets occupied by powerful brands supported by major, sophisticated manufacturers were thought to be protected by barriers of technology, money and marketing expertise. Laundry detergents is exactly such a market, dominated by Procter and Gamble and Lever Brothers in the UK (and in many other countries). Novon took on these giants, and was very successful, doubling Sainsbury's share of the field and taking one-fifth of the total detergent market in its stores, and up to a third of some sectors on a medium-term basis. It undercuts leading manufacturers' brands by 25 per cent, and clearly delivers at least adequate cleaning quality to its buyers.

It may be argued that Sainsbury shoppers are a particular type, and own-label detergent buyers a specific segment within that. There may be some truth in that, but there are clear lessons for manufacturers – and unpleasant ones at that.

First, Sainsbury's had tried before with its Wash and Care range in the 1980s, but this had failed. The retailer learned from the failure, and for the Novon development concentrated on understanding consumers and their needs. They identified the functional and operational defects of their previous products as perceived by users (for example particle size), and developed the new range in the classic way refined by the major manufacturers.

Second, Sainsbury's uses partnership with suppliers to share the cost of such developments, so it does not necessarily have to become a quasi-manufacturer with all the attendant overheads to launch new ranges.

Finally, and most importantly, if the detergent market is susceptible to determined attack by retailers' brands, what market is safe?

Sainsbury's themselves argue that Novon is a logical development, and indeed that they have had sub-brands since 1906; it is merely a way of improving their offer to their consumers (and of course differentiating themselves from their competitors). For manufacturers, it is a warning.

Other interesting examples are provided by the W. H. Smith chain in the UK. Within fields such as stationery it has a very basic generic range, one or more named middle-market brands and is developing premium-named brands: in writing paper there are the WHS Writing Pad, WHS Quality Bond, Expressions and at the top of the range Hambledon. A not unrelated fact is that Basildon Bond, which used to be the dominant brand leader in this market, is now in less than 50 per cent of W. H. Smith stores, and may in the end disappear altogether. It is retailers such as this who say that branding for a manufacturer is an ineffective way of getting a product on to the shelf compared to letting the retailer do the work. Does a manufacturer need a consumer marketing department when the retailer is closer to the market and knows so much better what consumers want?

This underlines the lesson which manufacturers must absorb: retailers' brands are no longer just cheap imitations, giving them a bit of extra margin, but part of their overall competitive strategy. For manufacturers this is a touchstone of their attitude: do they really accept and believe in this change? Some manufacturers certainly appear not to, and they seem almost to feel that retailers have no right to such pretensions. This is ostrich behaviour of the worst sort. The new power of retailers is a reality which cannot be shrugged off; their growing sophistication and strategic thinking must be accepted by their suppliers as here to stay.

As part of the process of understanding their customers discussed in Chapter 3, manufacturers must identify the strategy adopted by each, and the part played in it by the retailers' brands. Retailers are locked in a fiercely competitive struggle, many of them in essentially low- or no-growth markets. Although they can claim to be close to the consumer, they have relatively limited scope within which to differentiate themselves from competitors. In particular, they cannot use manufacturers' brands to do so except on price, and apart from discounters for whom low price is the strategy, most would rather not compete too fiercely on price alone. Other elements such as design and location are clearly important, but can usually be copied or improved on.

Retailers' brands therefore become one of the major ways in which they can try to make themselves unique. As with manufacturers, me-too products with nothing different to offer to consumers do not do this job of differentiation. The retailer is faced with exactly the same task as the manufacturer – understanding consumers in depth, identifying their wants and needs in a particular product field, anticipating changes in wants, and developing brands which are significantly different from others and which offer the right set of benefits to consumers. This is precisely what some retailers are already doing.

> Dixons is a major UK photographic, audio and video retailer. Using its own brand names, Saisho and Miranda, it offers a range of products unique to itself with, where possible, a differentiating feature such as graphic equalizers on personal stereos. The range offers value for money, but also a reasonable level of quality; it is designed to offer consumers an additional reason to shop in Dixons rather in competitors.

> Wickes is positioned at the heavy end of the DIY market, and deliberately tries to avoid direct competition with the mass-market retailers such as B & Q or Do-It-All. It tries to identify market opportunities within which it can offer a distinctive product. It entered the power tool market only when it found a gap for a hammer drill somewhere between the light consumer type and the very heavy-duty industrial product; the drill is sold under the Wickes name and carries a lifetime guarantee.

These examples suggest how some major retailers are now operating. A successful new retailers' brand will not only be profitable in its own right, but it will bring more people to the stores and reflect favourably on the overall image. Conversely, a poor brand will affect the consumers' perception in the wrong direction. The whole range of brands offered is vital to the retailer's success; within the overall strategy the private brands offer flexibility both as to the proportion devoted to private brands and to the width and depth of the private brand range.

The task of developing genuinely new and different brands is not becoming easier, either for manufacturers or for retailers. This leads inevitably to situations where successful new brands are followed by imitations; so far it is normally a manufacturer's brand imitated by a retailer's, but the first retailers' brands to be imitated by manufacturers have already appeared (such as Sainsbury's Vitapint). We are not talking about deliberate faking or pirating, which are real problems for some manufacturers but which are clearly illegal; the issue is imitations which are so close as to be almost indistinguishable from the original. Timotei, for example, has been one of the most successful new brands for many years in most European countries. Previously there had been no shampoos in white bottles, but soon retailers' brands appeared which looked almost identical to Timotei in colour, shape and graphics. This situation, and it is by no means unique, is particularly sensitive for manufacturers: it is difficult to accuse a retailer who accounts for a very substantial proportion of your business of plagiarism, still less to threaten legal action for passing off. On the other hand, the manufacturer must make the customer see that some imitations are just too close; the valuable brand property must be protected. As a senior manager in Elida Gibbs said of the Timotei situation, 'Well of course Boots are very good friends of ours: we're talking to them. . . .'

From the manufacturers' point of view, the challenge is to see how the consumer market is developing, how the various retailers are reacting and what strategy each is using, and to determine how his or her brands fit in both with market needs and with retailers' plans. This will lead to a fundamental decision – to manufacture retailers' brands or not.

To manufacture or not to manufacture retailers' brands?

Because of the competitive situation, and for the reasons outlined above, private brands will become more important for retailers. This does not necessarily mean that their share of all product fields will go on increasing ad infinitum. Penetration of retailers' brands will depend on a variety of factors – barriers to entry and exit, technology which can be protected, relative strength of manufacturers and retailers, consumer needs and so on. In supermarkets in both the USA and UK the overall share of packaged goods taken by retailers' brands is around 30 per cent and apparently stable (though this average figure covers huge variations). In other markets such as clothing it seems likely that retailers' brands will account for the majority of sales. Whatever the proportion, the retailers' brands will be strategically important to them, and therefore an issue in their relationships with suppliers.

If manufacturers take seriously the marketing principle that they should try to provide their customers with what they want, then they must at least face the decision as to whether or not to manufacture private brands for one or more of them. There is no doubt that that is what retailers want, and the better the manufacturers' brands (in uniqueness, quality or whatever), the more the retailers will want their own version. Taking the argument further, there is also no doubt that in most categories there is a segment of consumers who want retailers' brands. So doesn't it make sense to keep the customer happy, take advantage of profit opportunities and make retailers' brands?

Some manufacturers accept the argument, and do so. Some of course specialize in retailers' brands, and make a very good living at it: in the UK, S. R. Gent are an extremely successful supplier to Marks and Spencer, while Hillsdown Holdings have built up a large and very profitable business supplying retailers' brands in several food categories. Many manufacturers of well-known brand names also supply private label. Some, however, do not, and are firm (and loud) in their views as to why it is a mistake.

One of the best-known examples is Kellogg. Kellogg is one of the most successful and profitable consumer goods manufacturers in the world; their management of their markets and brands over the years in response to changing consumer tastes and retail structures contains lessons for every marketing manager. Their major brands are of a consistently superior quality to imitations, and they have supported them strongly. New brands have been developed to meet changing tastes and habits, and to fill segment gaps. Their proclamation that if it doesn't say Kellogg's on the pack, it isn't Kellogg's inside is a direct declaration of their belief in the quality of their product and a challenge to private-label products. The very strength of the brands and the high levels of marketing support mean that retailers are happy to continue to give large amounts of shelf space to the Kellogg brands.

These and other manufacturers who refuse to make retailers' brands argue that it is the only sensible policy; what brand manufacturers must be outstandingly good at is developing, manufacturing and sustaining brands, and anything else will detract from that concentration. Some go further and say that it is suicidal to manufacture for retailers: it is playing into their hands and will lead inevitably to greater retailer domination.

Others have taken a middle position and manufacture both for their brands and for retailers. A well-known example in the UK is United Biscuits, who rationalized their brands so that they could continue to support the strongest, and also make retailers' brands. Nabisco in the same market take a similar view.

Let us then look at how a manufacturer should approach the decision. There are a number of stages.

1 Do we have a choice?

The rigorous and objective analysis of the position of all your brands discussed in Chapter 2 should have told you whether you actually have a choice or not. The view which is now widely accepted is that all brands below number two in their product category will be de-listed, unless they have some real and continuing appeal to a significant segment of the market. Many manufacturers seem not to have grasped this, or they have a rosy view of their brands' real strengths and weaknesses.

At the very least, take a worst-case scenario as a possibility, and examine the effect on your business of losing distribution in multiples for a number of your brands. Such analysis must take account of technological change, consumer trends and competitive challenges from existing and new competitors, both manufacturers and retailers. If there is a sales and profit gap between what is left and what your company is looking for over the next few years, can you realistically fill the gap with new brands which you have the skills and resources to develop?

2 What is the capacity situation?

What is your production capacity, and what is the industry situation? In many sectors there is already overcapacity (in Europe as a whole if not in the UK), and in others the financial and technological barriers to entry are relatively low. In these circumstances the pressure to produce retailers' brands may become irresistible, both from the retailers themselves and from inside the company (both accountants and production people hate to see idle capacity!). Again the decision will be affected by your view as to the probability of being able to develop viable new brands yourself.

3 What are the company mission and culture?

These rather pompous jargon words reflect realities which will affect your decision. Some companies really see themselves as brand manufacturers, and any derogation from that as a betrayal of a sacred trust.

Senior and middle managers will have been raised on this view, and all their experience and skills will relate to a particular way of doing business; younger managers will have joined because of it. Changing a culture is slow and difficult. There is also the more pragmatic question of management skills.

4 Do we have the skills to make retailers' brands?

This may seem an odd question; after all, if you can make branded products, surely you can make own label? The question should perhaps be put more precisely, 'Can you make retailers' brands profitably?' This is different, for manufacturing retailers' brands demands different skills and priorities, perhaps different managers, from marketing manufacturers' brands.

5 If we do, what and for whom should we make?

There are a number of options here:

- Work only for one retailer, or for a preferred few, or for any.
- Work for a wholesaler or cash-and-carry group, or for a voluntary buying group.
- Make products identical to your existing brands (usually regarded as suicidal).
- Make products similar to, but slightly different from (inferior to?), your brands.
- Make products in the same field as your existing brands but different from anything you make now.
- Make new brands developed in collaboration with a retailer.

The choice made will depend on how much spare capacity is available; what economies of scale exist with your particular technology and plant; the relative strengths of you, your competitors and the retailers in this product field; what segments exist in consumer preferences and how well each is covered; and your strategy matched against those of your customers. There is also interaction between some of the options, and the final choice may be a combination of some of those listed.

Separate or integrated organization for retailers' brands?

Assuming that a manufacturer decides to make retailers' brands (or to continue doing so), it remains to work out how best to do it. The two basic options are to set up a separate organization to make and sell the retailers' brands, or to integrate manufacturers' and retailers' brands. Both types exist, and both seem happy with their own arrangement.

The arguments for integration are that a team should be trying to meet the needs of a market segment or category – the customers want retailers' brands as well as manufacturers' – therefore the same team should plan and deliver the complete range. This cuts out inefficiencies, overlap and wasteful competition.

The arguments against are that retailer pressure may make it appear easier to sell retailers' brands, and therefore the team will, over time, gradually lose its concentration on the manufacturer's brands, which are the source of the company's future strength. Competition between two operations, one making only manufacturers' brands and the other only retailers', will maximize market opportunities (a compromise would allow the same manufacturing plant but separate selling organizations).

The other argument for separation was mentioned above, that making retailers' brands calls for different attitudes and skills, and that therefore a specialist organization is needed. Clearly acting as a supplier, with the retailer doing all the market research and development, and making all the major decisions on product specification, means that the consumer marketing and the research and development departments are unnecessary. The manufacturer can concentrate on efficient production and delivery.

This is an oversimplification, of course. Even though companies such as Marks and Spencer and Sainsbury, who are regarded as leading exponents of retailers' brands, have massive development departments, it does not mean that their suppliers do not. Mainly the development work is collaborative, with the manufacturer carrying much of the responsibility. Experience in other fields, even the most technologically advanced, shows that the companies who succeed are truly market-oriented and take account of customer and consumer needs from an early stage of product development. The dichotomy between consumer-oriented and customer-oriented is false.

Manufacturers must find a solution which suits their particular situation. The existing organization, the breadth of the product range, the likely proportion of retailers' brands in the total mix, the number, size and location of production plants, all will have an influence on the decision. Longer-term planning will also take account of internationalization and its effects (see Chapter 10).

Summary

Retailers' brands are at the crux of the relationship between manufacturers and their customers. They raise basic questions as to:

- Who owns the consumer?
- Who owns the store?
- Who should control the marketing process?
- Who needs brands anyway?
- What exactly is a brand?

Retailers' brands are no longer just cheap, low-quality versions of
manufacturers' brands, but a legitimate part of the retailer's strategy, one
of the few ways they can develop uniqueness; many are regarded by
consumers as of at least equal quality to manufacturers' brands, and some
are seen as superior. The challenge to manufacturers is to predict how the
consumer market will change and to develop the brands which meet both
consumer and customer needs, and which retailers cannot copy easily.

A major question for manufacturers is whether or not to supply
retailers' brands. There are arguments for and against; probably only
those companies with the very strongest brands will be able to resist the
demand to manufacture for retailers.

Manufacturers should go through the decision process in a number of
stages:

1 Do we have a choice?
2 What is the capacity situation in the industry?
3 What is the company mission and culture?
4 Do we have the skills to make retailers' brands (as these are very
  different from those required for making national manufacturers'
  brands)?
5 If we do decide to make them, what brands should we produce and for
  whom?

A final decision is whether to have a separate organization for making
retailers' brands, or whether to integrate it with the main company. There
are arguments for both: integrating the two would allow the firm to
coordinate the needs of customers and consumers, to take an overall
market-led view of the category's needs; but meeting customers' needs
might appear easier, and detract from the single-minded concentration on
maintaining strong brands of your own.

5
Technology and information

The information technology (IT) revolution has affected many industries in dramatic ways. Its impact on retailing seems at first sight less profound, but this is a superficial view. Technologies which already exist have the potential to change some aspects of distribution out of all recognition. Whether or not they will – or rather, which changes will actually happen and which will not – is difficult to foresee. This chapter will describe briefly the possible developments which may occur, and then look in more detail at those which are already having an impact: electronic point of sale (EPOS), scanning, direct product profitability (DPP) and space management.

Potential impact of IT on retailing

One possible revolutionary development has been mentioned – armchair or tele-shopping. Combined with sophisticated direct marketing techniques this will enable retailers or manufacturers to customize product offers or even advertising to individuals based on an analysis of their previous purchasing and response to promotion. How widespread this will become will depend crucially on consumer response as well as on the technology and economics. Certainly the technology promises very sophisticated possibilities, and some futurists are certain that within the medium term whole areas of our lives will be transformed. Some scepticism is possible, however, as long as humans remain social animals and shopping in actual shops and shopping complexes offers them benefits which remote technology cannot match.

Apart from abolishing stores altogether, IT may radically alter what happens in the shops that remain. Current technology allows a multiple to change the price of a product at all its stores right across the USA at the touch of a button. A small module incorporating a display is fixed to the shelf under the product; the head office sends a radio message via satellite which tells the modules what price to display, and the same message changes the price in the store computer's look-up table for scanning.

Other possibilities affecting shoppers directly include self-scanning and in-store ATMs (cash dispensers). The development most likely to occur, though its timing and exact form remain unclear, is EPOS and electronic funds transfer at point of sale (EFTPOS). EPOS is already familiar and

---

The development of EPOS was a response to the retailer's need for accurate and up-to-date information on sales and stocks. This is needed not only for the basic decisions on merchandising, range, layout and so on, but also to cut shrinkage (from losses in the warehouse, in transfer to stores, in staff and public pilfering, and from till errors and 'sweethearting' or the practice of deliberately undercharging friends). Efficient nightly stock checks using hand-held electronic terminals allied to computerized inventory models could meet many of these needs, but a full EPOS system is even better. The most familiar system uses bar coding of every item (using standardized codes agreed by the Article Numbering Association, with compatible though not identical systems in the USA and Europe), read by a scanning device at the checkout – either a below-desk window or a wand or gun. Further developments have led to Traded Unit Coding in which outers or inner packs dealt with by wholesalers, cash-and-carry and retailers' warehouses can also be coded. An alternative code called ITF 14 based on the European Article Number structure is used, and is tolerant of printing on lower-grade packaging material. Some problems still exist with bar coding shrink-wrapped packs, but they will no doubt be solved.

Figure 5.1 EPOS

well-established in many if not most retail outlets: the old tills have been replaced by what are in effect computer terminals which not only produce the customer's bill but also record the data and accumulate them in a back-of-store computer. The implications of this are huge, and are treated later in this chapter. For the benefit of those unfamiliar with the details of EPOS a brief description is given in Figure 5.1; experts can skip this.

The advantages of EPOS have meant that it has been widely adopted not only by supermarkets but also (and in many cases earlier) by DIY outlets, department and variety stores, jewellers, clothing, furniture and stationery retailers, and fast food outlets. Not all use bar codes and scanning, but the principles and the benefits are the same. It seems probable that by the mid 1990s the great majority of packaged consumer goods will be sold through outlets with some form of EPOS.

EFTPOS (electronic funds transfer at point of sale) has been talked about for many years, but its installation has been delayed not only by the very large investment needed, but by problems of compatibility and, not least, by doubts as to consumer acceptance. The real benefits to consumers and to retailers themselves are not always clear. It seems likely at the time of writing that smart cards (which contain a small electronic chip) will eventually offer enough benefits (including data storage and transfer, and protection from fraud) to ensure their widespread acceptance.

Figure 5.2 EFTPOS

For manufacturers, these and other possible changes will have to be monitored carefully so that strategies can be developed to cope with new situations. It will not be enough to react after changes have already happened; the manufacturer who is ahead of the game will stay ahead, and will reap the rewards of being prepared.

The two areas in which it is already clear that major change has taken place and will continue are those of in-store automation and of information. The two are inter-related, and manufacturers must understand both.

In-store automation

The decreasing cost of hardware and the increasing availability of suitable software have meant that some retailers have applied computing power to a variety of in-store tasks. Examples from US supermarkets include:

- Order entry systems, front-end scanning, energy management systems.
- Meat, delicatessen scales and security systems.
- Automated receiving, time clocks and payroll.
- Baker and pharmacy systems, videotape rental systems.
- Customer enquiry terminals, video shopping terminals, electronic shelf tags; and so on.

A list of possible applications runs to over fifty items. As with other new developments in computing, there are problems of hardware and software reliability, compatibility of different systems, staff resistance, training and total costs. There is no doubt that competitive pressure will force more and more retailers to look to automation to reduce costs and improve efficiency; the question is not if but when each application will make its appearance in each retailer. Manufacturers must monitor these developments because they must continue to understand how they can fit in with the retailers' strategy and operations.

Obviously the area which most directly affects manufacturers is the order–delivery–invoicing interface. EPOS systems and scanning allow the retailer to keep very detailed track of precisely what is moving off the shelves/racks. An inventory control model can trigger automatic reordering when the computer shows that a given stock level has been reached. At the ultimate, the retailer's computer can be connected directly to the supplier's, and the reordering can take place with no human intervention at all (Figure 5.3).

The apparently simple and logical statements in Figure 5.3 hide a great deal of complication. As anyone at all familiar with computer systems will have recognized, there are likely to be a number of hurdles to be cleared before this level of integration can be achieved. An example will make this clearer:

Suppose that a supermarket in the USA is offered a special 'street money' deal from a DSD (direct store delivery) vendor for a display. The manager accepts the deal and lowers his retail price to match a competitor's. He must now change the files that involve at least two in-store systems. He must go

Connecting the computers of the supplier and retailer clearly offers enormous potential benefits. For the operation to work the two computer systems have to be able to communicate, and this demands a common 'language' – an electronic data interchange or EDI. Such a common standard has been developed, and EDI systems are now common; indeed, in some cases they are positively driving the development of wider cooperation between manufacturers and retailers. Interestingly, retailers see different benefits in the adoption of the system: some are looking for savings in staff needed to process orders, while others see benefits from reducing stockholding costs. EDI is currently well-established in basic applications in many fields, and will undoubtedly spread both more widely (to other manufacturers and retailers), and more deeply (to other applications within a manufacturer/retailer relationship, from ordering to invoicing and payment). As of January 1992, there were some 1800 manufacturer members of the INS Tradanet EDI system.

Figure 5.3 EDI

to his DSD files with the formats and data requirements of this application and enter the allowance and new retail price. Then he must change the retail price on his scanning system. Now half the work is done. Since this information was altered from within the store, the manager must change the files back to the original at the end of the promotion. While the DSD system might have an automatic change procedure, scanning systems do not. If the files also have a shelf label and sign printing application, the data might have to be entered four times to set up the deal and four times to remove it. This data management and control process is further complicated by the fact that each application may have its own data requirements, input screens and procedures. . . .

From *Supermarket Business* (USA) February 1987

Compatibility problems are aggravated by the fact that a mix of personal computers (PC)s, minis and mainframes are quite likely to be involved. PCs mostly operate at 1200 baud, while most scanning communications operate at 2400 baud. The Article Numbering Association introduced TRADACOMS (Trading Data Communications) standards which set out a procedure for structuring messages by organizing data in such a way that they could be applied regardless of computer make, size or model.

The food industry is moving towards a standard communications protocol (UCS or Universal Communications Standard) in the USA, and some such standardization is clearly desirable.

Another development in electronic data exchange is TRADANET, also supported by the Article Numbering Association (ANA). This system is an electronic mailbox which allows members to deliver and collect messages to and from their trading partners in complete security. The TRADANET system is now widespread in many industries and is used by thousands of companies both large and small; it seems certain to become the norm for many communications and transactions.

The average marketing or sales person may be forgiven for turning slightly pale at all this jargon. What has it got to do with us, after all? The whole point is that these developments in retailers necessarily affect suppliers. Manufacturers must understand the retailers' systems intimately so that they can not only respond to such issues, but can plan for them.

Which manufacturer is likely to get the warmer reception, the one who approaches the retailer with a proposition aware of and with helpful answers to the practical problems raised by its implementation, or the one who is surprised that it causes the retailer problems at all?

Difficulties for the computer-illiterate do not end there, for the biggest change concerns the information that retailers will have, and what they can do with it.

Information

EPOS provides many cost savings, both hard and soft, to retailers, but the main benefit to them will be in information. It may be seen that in principle an EPOS will provide disaggregated data on the sales of every item, including time and date. It will then be possible to calculate sales rates, stock levels, stock turn, price and margin at any time for each item, for categories, stores and so on almost ad infinitum.

It is said that one Dutch store manager uses data to put friendly, chatty till operators on duty while sales are slow, and faster, more efficient ones when sales speed up. I have personally seen a store manager querying why the bakery made sixteen Danish pastries yesterday when ten of them had to be price-reduced at 4 p.m. Virtually any analysis, from the most detailed to the most broad and high-level, is theoretically possible. This of course points to the central issue: can the retailer develop software which will reduce the enormous amount of data to a usable set of information? Moreover, will the staff be available and trained actually to use it?

It seems clear that even if the process is slow at first, most retailers will soon have a grip of their EPOS data, and that this will theoretically be an enormous advantage to them. The question as to who owns the data has been raised by manufacturers, as their exclusion from its use would handicap them in negotiation. Traditionally, manufacturers could argue that only they really understood the consumer, and that therefore the retailer ought to listen to their arguments. Now retailers can and do argue that it is they who have all the information.

In fields in which article numbering applies, there is an obligation on retailers to give access to 'basic data' from scanning at cost. Currently retailers are interpreting this strictly, and giving out very little, or are trying to sell the data at high prices. The move towards market research companies acting as central buyers and then syndicating reports is probably the way forward, although even with widespread availability of such services it is not clear that manufacturers will have access to the information they really need.

Manufacturers in packaged goods fields have relied for many years on retail audits to provide them with vital data on what is happening within the distribution channel. It now seems likely that these sources will be superseded by scanner data, which should be much more accurate, efficient and timely. What they may not provide is information on sales by identified retailers – and that is precisely what manufacturers increasingly want.

Manufacturers are therefore in a dilemma: they must buy whatever scanner data are made available, just so that they can talk to customers on more or less equal terms; but the retailers will always know more about their own sales, and published scanning data will not give manufacturers the vital information on performance within competing multiples.

Let us look in more detail at the implications of EPOS data, and how it will affect the relationship between suppliers and retailers.

Retailers will now be able to measure precisely the effect on sales of a large number of variables – price, number of facings, shelf position, position in store, pack size, number of sizes and varieties, promotions, even advertising. Some of these will be more complicated and difficult to measure than others, but retailers will always be in a better position than manufacturers to attempt to quantify effects. When DPP measures are built in (see below), the effects on contribution to store profits can be gauged, and may provide the retailer with arguments which the manufacturer will find very hard to meet. Knowledge is power, and this trend is once again transferring power from manufacturers to retailers.

An allied effect is on promotional activity in general. For some years there has been a trend for total promotional spending to move more below-the-line, that is, for a decreasing proportion to be spent on main media advertising. This is in itself a reflection of retailer power, of course. The extra effect of EPOS is that retailers will accept only promotions which can be handled easily within the constraints of their system. Thus, if a promotional pack has to have a separate bar code, this has cost and hassle implications for retailers, and they may refuse certain promotions purely because of EPOS-related handling considerations. It is fair to say, on the other hand, that EPOS will make some types of promotion easier, for example 'Buy four, get one free'; the computer can be programmed to charge the fifth pack at zero, no matter what order items are presented in. These multi-buy promotions are often extremely successful, and are increasing rapidly in many sectors. Coupons can be bar coded and can then be scanned easily (though this does not solve the problem of retailers who announce that they will redeem any coupon as cash against any purchase, not just the designated brand).

On the product itself, EPOS will have little direct effect except that mentioned above, of retailer knowledge of what variety, pack size etc. actually sell. The effect on packaging is more direct, since it is up to the manufacturers to ensure that the correct bar code is printed in a way which makes it easily readable. The Article Numbering Association has recommendations on how to achieve this on various different types of pack. On small packs, the general problem of how to achieve impact on the shelf or rack is made worse by having to include the bar code, particularly as many packs are now printed in several languages. Although this is all a challenge for the designers, there is no sign that it is an insuperable one.

The lesson for manufacturers is always understanding and sensitivity: understand what is happening in the retailer, and the implications of the new systems; be sensitive to the impact your actions have on the systems. Decisions which used to be taken by manufacturers entirely within their own organization and without thought for their implications for anyone except the consumers now have to be considered in the light of retailers' needs too. The whole series of processes which the product will go through between the factory gate and the consumer's home now has to be thought through by the manufacturer before decisions are taken.

This leads neatly into the idea of DPP.

DPP

DPP can be used both by manufacturers to examine costs in their end of the distribution chain and by retailers to look at theirs, and of course by

The idea of DPP has been around for some time, and is basically just applied management accounting: in looking at the contribution of a product to total company overhead and profit, all costs attributable to it should be counted. In retailing terms, it has been customary to look at the basic figure of price and gross margin: the profitability can then be calculated either as a percentage, or as the total profit generated by a measured shelf/rack space.
DPP goes further than this, by pointing out that products use resources such as back-of-store space, staff handling time and so on. A true profitability calculation must take account of these, since they may vary between products in unforeseen ways. Just as one product may have a lower gross margin than another, but make up for it by selling at a faster rate, so one product may look more profitable than another until one takes into account that it takes up much more space in the warehouse or has to be handled three times against the other's once.

Like many simple ideas, DPP was easier to describe than to implement. The sheer volume of data and calculation required meant that early work in the 1960s in the USA by consultants, manufacturers and retailers came to little. The advent of scanning and cheap computing power changed the picture, and in the early 1980s Procter and Gamble and McKinsey's produced a model which was workable. More general interest led to a unified approach led by the Food Marketing Institute, which produced a PC-based model using Lotus 1-2-3 in 1985. Similar models were later developed in the UK and elsewhere. Some retailers developed their own models particularly adapted to their trade or situation, and naturally were reluctant to publish details. As of the late 1980s it can be stated that any manufacturer or retailer interested could gain access to a DPP model fairly easily.

Figure 5.4 DPP

both to try to estimate costs and profits in the other's field to use in negotiation. Again, knowledge is power, and manufacturers must be in a position to use information or combat argument. We shall therefore look at DPP in a little more detail before going on to see how the two parties use the output.

Ideally DPP would take account of every cost incurred by each separate SKU (stocking unit, such as one pack size of one variety of one brand). There is disagreement about the precise level of detail on cost which is necessary and practical; whether every separate action at every stage needs to be timed and costed, or whether broad summaries of each stage are sufficient. For our purposes it is enough to state that each stage in the progress of a product must be identified and costed. Normally these can be split into transport, warehouse and store.

Imagine all the stages a typical packaged product goes through: usually it will be packed in outers; loaded on to pallets; assembled in a goods outwards area; loaded on to a lorry; transported to a warehouse; unloaded and stored for a varying length of time; possibly broken up into different assortments; reloaded on a pallet; loaded on to a lorry; transported to a retail store; unloaded and perhaps moved to a back store; broken up and stacked on shelves; it will then occupy a varying amount of shelf or rack space for a varying length of time.

All these activities cost money, and the nature of products (size, shape, density), width and depth of range (number of sizes, flavours or colours), selling characteristics (high or low turnover), number of facings, price and margin will all potentially affect the DPP.

It is of course unrealistic for either a manufacturer or a retailer to try simply to minimize each cost, since many of the objectives involved in the system conflict. For example, minimizing transport and handling costs by using only full container loads may increase the time that some products stay in the warehouse; minimizing warehouse stock may increase stock-outs in the shop and therefore lose profit opportunities.

What DPP can do is identify costs so that they can be fed into decisions. Although most of the comment on DPP has focused on retailers, it can also be of direct value to manufacturers, sometimes by revealing unexpected or unknown facts. For example, one very sophisticated manufacturer allowed a discount on a full container load of one size of a brand. This was based on the 'knowledge' that the factory produced one size at a time; costs between the production line and the container would therefore be minimized by loading only one size at a time. In fact, a DPP investigation led the Sales Director to the discovery that the factory produced the three sizes simultaneously! The price list was changed, in a way which made it easier for customers to order, and at no extra cost to the manufacturer. There is a lesson here which goes beyond just DPP (and which will be returned to in the discussion of organization design in Chapter 8).

Let us now look at the results of DPP studies and the implications for manufacturers. The most important result of all studies reported is that

Gross margin for the retailer is the difference between the price at which an item is bought and the price at which it is sold; if it is bought at 85p per unit and sold for £1, the gross margin is 15p or 15 per cent. The retailer also takes account of the rate of sale, since some products sell much faster than others. All other things being equal, the retailer tries to maximize the combination of gross margin and rate of sale.

DPP takes account of the fact that all other things are not equal, and that the costs of storage, handling and shelf space, for example, vary between products. Building in all relevant direct product costs may produce a quite different picture from that shown by simple gross margin calculations. For example, take two products – A and B – with identical gross margins and sales rates. A, however, because of its pack design, or the way it fits into the outers or trading units, takes up more space in the warehouse and on the shelf, and also takes slightly longer to handle in store. The calculations might then show:

	Product A	Product B
Retail price	1.00	1.00
Buying-in price	85	85
Gross margin	15	15
Direct product costs		
Warehouse	5	3
Handling	3	2
Shelf space	2	1
Total DPC	10	6
DPP	5	9

What this means is that it may be dangerous to rely on simple measures such as gross margin, which may actively mislead decisions on buying and space allocation.

Figure 5.5 DPP and gross margin

there is no correlation between DPP and gross margin (Figure 5.5). This is a significant finding for retailers, who mainly make decisions on gross margin data. Indeed, one study found that some 20 per cent of supermarket products have a negative DPP...'which shows how inaccurate gross margins can be for making merchandising decisions. Many of the lowest DPP items are those that you're promoting most often, which means you're losing money with every additional case you sell.'

For manufacturers, the point is that if DPP is widely adopted, its output may affect decisions on the stocking, store position and pricing of their brands, as well as on the terms demanded by customers. Some manufacturers are using the approach in a pro-active way to help their customers as well as themselves.

Procter and Gamble in the USA claims that it may modify packaging, case packs, pallet configuration, discount structures and other variables on the basis of DPP analyses.

Offering increased profitability in this way has more impact than higher allowances or more promotions because it affects the bottom line directly – while also preserving P and G's margins. Examples are:

- Increasing the density of laundry detergent reduced the cube size by 15 per cent and increased the number of units per case from twelve to fourteen; lower handling costs resulted in savings of 26 cents per case.
- Changing the shape of the Downy (fabric conditioner) bottle resulted in packaging efficiencies with savings of 35 cents per case.
- Knowing that up to 62 per cent of DPP costs were cube related, they analysed the way Crisco was packed. The contents of the bottles filled only 26 per cent of the outer case. P and G redesigned the bottle in a similar shape but with a less narrow waist, and used plastic instead of glass. The result was a reduction in costs of 32 cents per case for the retailer.
- The Ivory shampoo bottle was changed to a 'value-for-money' cylinder. The danger was that brand loyalty would be lost; in fact the brand gained wider consumer appeal and 29 cents per case reduction in costs.

The last example points up the central dilemma for the manufacturer: DPP or other cost considerations must always be put into the context of the brand and its consumers. Savings for the retailer, and even for the manufacturer, are irrelevant if they detract from the brand's consumer appeal.

How DPP is used by retailers and manufacturers

Since the majority of handling costs are at the retailer end of the channel, and since handling and storage costs form the majority of the 'hidden' costs identified by DPP, it should follow that retailers are the main users. It is true that some retailers, such as Safeway in the USA, are major users of DPP, and others in Europe are thought to be. Most large UK grocery multiples now use DPP fairly routinely, either working with the standard industry model or developing their own; other retailers such as W. H. Smith have their own model, but elsewhere use is much more patchy. The reasons can be deduced from the nature of the task: it demands large volumes of data, much of which have not previously been collected, some computer software, and the people to run the models and interpret the results. Taking these demands together, it is not surprising that retailers have not yet applied DPP to all their thousands of products. Safeway's secret seems to be in having a fairly automated system which uses a relatively broad-brush approach to costs.

The only UK retailer generally thought to have applied DPP rigorously is Boots (dominant in ethical and over-the-counter pharmaceuticals, a major force in toiletries, and now also in many other product fields). It is thought that Boots has applied DPP rigidly, for example dropping the whole category of pet foods because it showed a DPP loss despite making three-quarters of a million pounds gross profit. Manufacturers feel that they are put into a difficult position because Boots has high staff and distribution costs, which are then automatically loaded on to all products by DPP. This points up again the need to be aware of the use of DPP and to have sufficient expertise in it to be able to argue about the results of analysis, even though the retailer holds the whip hand because he or she has the data.

In some fields manufacturers have taken the lead in introducing DPP, and the largest fmcg producers have mostly developed some capacity to handle it. The motivation has sometimes been pro- active, as in Procter and Gamble's case, but has also often been defensive: 'The argument may be used against me, so I'd better be prepared.' For some time it appeared that some manufacturers both in the USA and in Europe held the edge over some retailers in the ability to use sophisticated models. This has changed, and leading retailers are now expert. At present the use of DPP results by retailers in negotiation occurs rarely, though it is present as a background factor. Many cases are found in which a manufacturer and a particular retailer will work together on a DPP analysis of a category.

This points up both the opportunity for manufacturers and the difficulty they once again have with access to information. The commonly available DPP models use 'standard industry data' for certain cost elements, and manufacturers must make do with these unless retailers will cooperate and give their own costs. Such cooperation does happen, on both sides of the Atlantic. Clearly it will be to manufacturers' benefit if greater industry cooperation does produce commonly accepted figures with which both partners can work.

Space management systems

If DPP is a help to understanding the real contribution from different products, it is only one input to the complex decisions facing retailers. Competitive pressure and increasing costs of land, buildings, labour, energy and so on mean that decisions on what exactly to stock and how to allocate space in the store have become crucial. This has always been so, and it might be argued that this is the core skill of retailing. Added to the high cost of space and the ever-increasing number of products, there are now other pressures such as the decreasing number of shopping trips, changing customer expectations and the need to project a coherent and relevant store image. Merchandising decisions are now more complex as well as more crucial than ever. Since the decisions are what manufacturers most want to influence, it is vital to them to understand how retailers are tackling the problem.

As with DPP, the availability of computing power and EPOS data has brought new methods of analysis to help in complex decision making; software packages can be used in what are called space management or space allocation systems. What they try to do is to systematize what the merchandising decision maker is doing, and to perform many times over the calculations which help in the decision making.

Consider the decisions which have to be made, and the influences on them:

- Which categories shall we stock?
- How much space should be allocated to each?
- How should this vary between different stores in the group?
- How should the categories be arranged through the shop, so that dead zones are avoided, and consumers are routed past most or all categories without boring or frustrating them?
- What service level should be set for each product (per cent of shoppers looking for an item who find it in stock)?

- How do sales of each product fluctuate over time?
- How much space should be allocated to each SKU (item of stock) in order to meet the different objectives of customer satisfaction, minimum labour cost, maximum sales and profit?
- What is the effect of varying range and variety on sales and profit?
- What is the effect of one product on sales of the adjoining ones?
- What is the minimum stock that needs to be held for each SKU, given service level and safety stock requirements, uncertainty of forecasts, and order/delivery times?
- What is the optimum order time and size, given the above and the manufacturer's discount structure and any deals on offer?

There are probably other factors, but this is enough to show how complicated the decisions are. Experience has provided guidelines, and most retailers will have certain rules which cut down the complexity, while common sense also helps: for example, no product over a certain weight on the highest shelf, or no small cubic size packs on the very large bottom shelf. Beyond that, what has in the past been done manually or with a lot of work with the calculator can now be done with the help of a space management package.

Some retailers have developed their own, but there are commercial packages which are in widespread use by both retailers and manufacturers, the best-known being Spaceman II/Spacemax, accuSPACE, and Apollo. All run on IBM-compatible microcomputers, use broadly similar input and procedures and produce broadly similar output, although there are of course differences between them. An outline of the process is shown in Figure 5.6.

A number of points can be made about space management systems. First, they undoubtedly offer very welcome help to retailers in making a series of complex decisions; like most computer packages, they can make hundreds of routine calculations easily and quickly, calculations which otherwise might not get done.

Second, they still rely on a considerable amount of human judgement for input. Because output comes from a computer and looks impressive, we are sometimes tempted to give it more credence than it deserves. In the case of space management models, it is extremely important to understand exactly what has gone on in the model, and to be aware of what impact assumptions and judgement have on the results. Changing key assumptions and inputs can change the results significantly; if these include recommendations on varying space allocation for your products, or dropping one or more, you will need to be able to challenge them!

Although the models appear complicated at first, they are in fact simple; essentially, they repeat a basic process for each SKU. Although they can be applied to whole categories across a store, it is more normal to take one category at a time and to explore differing arrangements within that category. Often this means looking at one fixture such as a gondola in a supermarket. The steps are as follows.

1 For each SKU determine the inventory requirement. This can be done subjectively, based on experience, by using one of the defaults set in the model such as 1½ cases, or 3 days' supply; or by using a sub-model. The last will make explicit what is implicit in a human judgement, taking into account such factors as sales pattern, uncertainty of sales forecast, order/delivery sales lead time, and service level.

2 Policy decisions can be input, specifying which products are allowed on each shelf (e.g. no pack over 10 lb weight above shoulder height).

3 Judgements may be quantified on, for example, the relative effect of different shelf positions on the different products, and the effect of adjacent products on each other. Such judgements can of course be based on hard evidence from experiments tracked by scanning or other EPOS systems.

4 The model then tries to meet the inventory requirement goal for each product, to allocate each to the best shelf position, and to evaluate the effect of a particular pattern of allocation.

5 Normally the model will rank all products in descending order on a criterion selected by the operator. This will be one or a combination of such variables as:

- Sales in dollars or appropriate currency.
- Gross profit.
- Gross profit return on inventory investment (ROII).
- DPP.
- DPPROII (using average inventory).

A criterion may be expressed in terms of linear or cubic space, e.g. gross profit per cubic foot.

6 The programme will either describe the effect of a particular layout chosen by the operator in terms of the chosen criteria,

or will try to find some recommended mix. In the latter case, products lower down in the ranking may be dropped from the space completely either because the shelves are all full before it is reached in the list, or because the recommended facings are less than some predetermined minimum (e.g. two packs).

7 Output will consist of a series of tables listing the products with accompanying statistics on costs, prices, margins, ROII etc., and a graphic representation of the fitment as filled in the chosen or recommended way. This planogram can be made up of line drawings of actual pack outlines, or may in the more sophisticated versions produce full colour simulations of what that display would look like; examples of tabular and graphic output are shown in Figures 5.7–5.9. Many other analyses and outputs are usually available.

Figure 5.6 Space management models

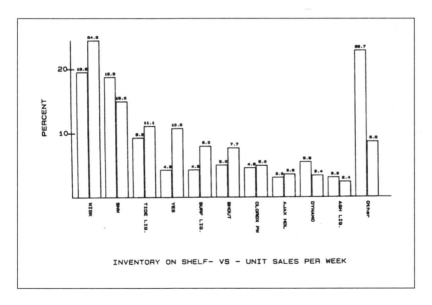

Figure 5.7 Ingles HDL detergents current 12 ft

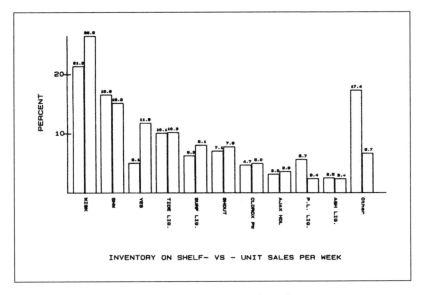

Figure 5.8   Ingles HDL detergents proposed 12 ft option A

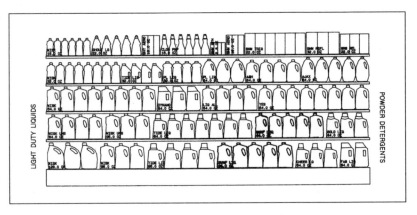

Figure 5.9   Ingles HDL detergents proposed 12 ft option A

Use by retailers and manufacturers

At the time of writing some retailers are making considerable use of space management models; many, however, would admit that they do not use them as much as they might; some do not use them at all. The reason is easy to see: even with the help of the computer, a very large amount of work can be involved, and much of it demands a reasonably high level of skill and experience. With the range of products found in many stores, it would take a huge amount of person-hours to produce results for the whole business. Of course, over time a considerable body of knowledge can be built up; not all categories have to be re-planned from scratch every week. Leading retailers now use space management as they use DPP - routinely.

Some manufacturers have been involved with the models from an early stage; most reasonably progressive companies have at least bought one or more of the best-known packages and have made sure that someone understands them. In some cases they have gone further and set up a unit which specializes in space management, and which will produce analyses either for the company itself or for a cooperating retailer. Clearly the issue of availability of data raises itself again, and the models can really be run successfully only with retailer help.

Manufacturers need to understand space management models for defensive reasons – so that they can deal with decisions by retailers based on them. But again they can use them in a proactive way. Since some retailers do not use the models as much as they could, because of a shortage of skilled people, the manufacturer can offer to help. More, they can put themselves forward as category expert: although they would never try to teach the customer his or her business, they can claim to know more about their own particular category than the retailer can hope to.

With the increasing pressure on space, retailers will be looking actively to drop products. Manufacturers on the other hand want to extend their existing product range and to introduce new products: they will have to have very strong arguments for either, and increasingly will need to base their own argument on a detailed space management analysis. Procter and Gamble, for example, did this when introducing boy and girl Pampers (disposable nappies); the number of SKUs and the amount of space needed both increased with the new range, and the presentation showed how the retailers would benefit through suitable space allocation.

The future – integrated systems

At present, the different computer-based packages used in retailing are frequently completely separate; even the space management models are often not linked to DPP data, although that would be the most logical thing to do. In theory, all the different systems should be linked, both within each store and throughout the company. Some packages do exist which offer integrated accounting and merchandise control. One such – Retail Interact – offers:

- Links to EPOS and scanning.
- Inventory and sales performance by category.
- Price ticket generation.
- Price change control.
- Open-to-buy forecasting and planning.
- Store transfers.
- Back door control.
- Invoicing and cash control.
- Salesperson performance control.

The system is claimed to be suitable for electrical goods, shoes, fashion, department stores, DIY and home improvement, hard goods, and wines and spirits amongst others.

As retailers continue to become more sophisticated and to develop their in-house staff, they will undoubtedly make more use of IT. Manufacturers will have to continue to keep up with these developments if they are to be able to hold a dialogue, let alone to influence decisions in the way they wish.

Summary

Technology has already had a considerable impact on retailing and will have more in the future. Developments such as tele-shopping, combined with data-base marketing, may offer whole new channels. EPOS and EFTPOS are being installed rapidly, and manufacturers must understand their implications for retailers and for their own relationship with them.

In-store automation is likely to develop fast; more than fifty applications are already possible. Manufacturers must monitor these as they are installed so that they can actively plan their operations to take account of them.

The centre of the relationship is at the order–delivery–invoicing interface. EDI and associated developments such as TRADACOMS and TRADANET are driving the demand for closer cooperation between supplier and customer. The manufacturer who plans for these developments rather than reacting to them will gain an advantage.

Perhaps the major effect of technology, especially of EPOS and scanning, will be on the information available to retailers. Issues raised include:

- Who owns the data?
- The effect on the balance of power.
- The impact on what promotions are accepted.

Manufacturers must try to make sure that they obtain access to the enormously rich data which scanning will produce.

DPP is important to manufacturers both for their own use and because retailers will be using it. Although it is used little in negotiations at present, this may change, and manufacturers must be prepared so that they can use it both positively and defensively.

There is little correlation between DPP and gross margin; up to 20 per cent of supermarket products may have negative DPP. If used by retailers such calculations would have serious implications for manufacturers.

Some manufacturers are already using DPP in a proactive way, for example in redesigning packs and pallet and outer configurations.

Space management models are a welcome aid to retailers in making complicated decisions on merchandising. They still rely on subjective inputs, and it is vital that manufacturers understand the assumptions and process being used. Some manufacturers offer help to customers in using space management models for particular categories. All manufacturers, and especially the people dealing with customers, must understand the models so that they can respond to negotiating positions based on them.

In future, integrated systems may develop which tie together all the separate IT applications. It will be even more important for manufacturers to keep abreast of these, as they could affect major policy decisions by retailers.

6
Bringing the information together

It should be clear by now that in order to work more effectively with customers a supplier has to bring a considerable amount of information to bear. Much of it will be available already, though perhaps not in the right form, and not in the right place at the right time; other data may not be available, and decisions will have to be taken as to whether and how to collect them.

The form in which information is stored and disseminated is less important than purposeful planning to ensure that the people who need data can find what they want when they want it. There is no doubt, however, that the availability of relatively cheap computing power has made an enormous difference to the potential storage and use of data. Unfortunately, the potential has all too often been oversold, and surrounded by opaque jargon. So far we have been offered MIS (management information systems or marketing information systems), DSS (decision support systems) and other acronyms; now we have MSP (marketing and sales productivity). The golden promise of such systems has all too often not been met, or met only after enormous expenditures of time and money.

While we should be sceptical, however, we should not be cynical. The marketing task depends crucially on information, and this dependence is increasing. The ability to bring information to bear in dealing with customers offers opportunities for real strategic advantage. This means that the issue must be tackled at two levels. Top management must look seriously at the information needs of the company as a whole. They must not, as they have in the past, delegate to the 'experts', but must grapple with the technology themselves. As a leading American chief executive (of a subsidiary of Rockwell) said, 'If you can't understand the fundamentals of a technological decision, you're a figurehead. You're not the CEO.' To implement serious computer-based information systems demands the commitment of serious money; this must be an informed board decision.

At the functional level, sales and marketing people must also take responsibility for getting the information they want. For some reason, many of them at present are still computer-phobic. This is changing rapidly, but the process needs to go faster in many companies. Those which do not get to grips with current technology will lose ground to competitors, and control to customers. The size of the opportunity is underlined by claims that manufacturers' service activities account for 75 to 85 per cent of all value added. 'This means that the price a product can command is less a reflection of raw materials and labour than of marketing-related services like selecting appropriate product features, determining the product mix and ensuring product availability and delivery.' (Moriarty, *Harvard Business Review* Jan–Feb 1989.) Information systems which help to improve the efficiency and effectiveness of marketing activities can therefore have a direct impact on the bottom line.

Obviously the way a particular company approaches the problem will depend on its size and resources. Even though computer hardware is fairly cheap, software, communications and liveware (or people, as they used to be called) are still expensive. Each firm must match its ambition to its pocket; appropriate and useful systems can be built for quite small sums. To repeat, it is the quality of thinking and planning which is important, rather than the sophistication of the technology.

Let us therefore look at the information we need to bring together, both from within the company and from outside. The information is grouped in the following way:

Internal
- Accounting
  Product profitability
  Customer profitability
  Budgets and reports
  Sales forecasting

- Production

External
● Markets
● Consumers
● Customers
● Competitors

Internal

Accounting information

Much of the information we need from inside the company is about costs, revenue and profit. It comes from the accounting system, and therein lies a problem. Accountants produce data for their own purposes and according to their own rules and conventions. This is right and proper, but it can mean that what they produce is not appropriate for other users. This is not an accounting text, but one or two general remarks are relevant.

First, costing systems are necessarily artificial. They estimate and allocate costs to products, but however sophisticated the system, some allocations are made arbitrarily. Important decisions are made on the basis of the figures produced, for example on which products are more or less profitable and therefore which should be supported or dropped. Such comparisons are reliable only to the extent that the underlying costs are reliable, and it is known that they are accurate only in certain fairly restrictive conditions. For example, overheads are often allocated according to volume of production. As long as volume varies relatively little between products, cost estimates will be fairly accurate. This accuracy falls off rapidly as the ratio of volume goes from 5 to 1 to 10 to 1. Again, overheads may be allocated on the basis of labour costs; with increasing automation this may become decreasingly accurate (Figure 6.1).

Second, and this remark could perhaps stand for the chapter as a whole, all information itself carries a cost – that is, it costs money to collect, store and retrieve. There is a limit to how much it is worth spending on information. Having no information would be enormously risky, if not suicidal. At the other extreme it is possible to have more data than anyone can handle, or to spend more on it than can be recovered. Deciding how much is enough can be a complex problem (interested readers are referred to books on Bayesian decision analysis; see the reading list), but there are some rules of thumb:

The attack on conventional management accounting has been led by a Harvard Business School professor, Robert Kaplan. He pointed out, for example, that in one factory direct labour accounted for just 4 per cent of total costs; yet 65 per cent of the plant's cost system focused on direct labour. Kaplan argues that obsolete accounting systems lead to a dangerous misallocation of resources. Wrong decisions based on wrong data – on what products are profitable, which to support and which to drop, what prices to charge – could mean a loss of competitiveness.

The answer is to identify what factors really influence the cost of making and selling a product – the cost drivers. This approach is known as activity analysis; the analogy with DPP is clear, and it seems very relevant to the analysis of customer profitability too. For further details of Kaplan's work, see the reading list at the end of this chapter. (Johnson *et al.* 1987).

Figure 6.1 Activity costing

- What decisions do I need to make? Decisions on resource allocation to different brands have been mentioned. Others will include such matters as what discount structure to adopt (or accept).
- What would I do differently if I had that information? Some information has what a former boss of mine used to call 'a high so-what value': interesting, but it makes no difference to what you do. This test applies to information which you collect for decision making or control purposes ('Should I do A or B?', or 'Is it all going according to plan?').
- How could I use it in working with customers? This may cover both offensive and defensive uses, that is information which you use in a positive way to help sell your brands, or which you collect to be able to defend yourself against negative arguments.
- Another rule might be: Are my competitors using it, and if so, what advantage are they getting from it? The other two rules still apply, since our competitors are not always right.

Armed with these rules, then, let us look at what we may ask our accountants to provide.

Product profitability

This information is central to basic marketing decisions. The caveats entered above are most important here, as misleading figures on relative profitability can lead to mistaken strategic choices. Although I would take it as axiomatic that any company knows where it makes its money, in practice some accounting systems give only a rough guide, or indeed none at all. One very well-known food manufacturer used until very recently a standard percentage cost figure for all its many products: the resulting information on product profitability was therefore completely useless in making decisions on resource allocation, as it could have been very misleading as to where profits were actually being made.

Knowing the contribution and profit margins of each brand (and indeed pack size and variety) is fundamental, even though it does not necessarily lead in a simple way to clear decisions. Less profitable brands or varieties can justify their existence because they are part of a range which customers or consumers demand, for example. Having said all that, managers must know which brands, sizes etc. are making what profits so that they can take sensible decisions on how to allocate resources, and what will be the profit impact of different strategies.

Customer profitability

It should follow that if a company adopts a customer orientation, it also needs data on customer profitability. Many manufacturers have moved or are moving in this direction, though some very sophisticated ones are not. The reason for this surprising resistance is a result of the 'What would I do with it if I had it?' rule. Companies who have decided not to analyse profitability by customer (and I exclude those who simply haven't thought about it) argue that they already try to maximize profit from each account anyway: what would they do differently if they knew that they were making 15 per cent from customer A and only 12 per cent from customer B? This could of course also apply to product profitability. It can be contrasted with the other extreme.

H. J. Heinz were one of the earliest adopters of a trade marketing approach in the UK. They produce customer profitability figures which show not only the normal allocations of manufacturing and administration costs, but also detailed cost of sales force effort; real costs of visits, presentations and national account manager time are recorded and allocated. As a result they have a very clear idea of how much they are making from each customer, and

can take action accordingly. As with brand profitability, this does not mean
that they will stop doing business with a customer who is less profitable than
the average or target (especially if it happens to be one of the largest). It can
affect the allocation of resources to customers, either in promotional budgets
or in sales force effort. Customer profitability data can show that it is simply
not worth putting that amount of effort into a particular account, or that it
would be worth switching resources from one to another.

The collection of this sort of data – called in a broader sense activity value
analysis – can lead to a radical reappraisal of the sales force. Good hard
data on product mix profitability by account can be used to attack the
long tail of the sales force, of distributors and of products themselves. The
sorts of questions to be asked are:

- What are we actually getting out of this particular combination of
  products and customers?
- Do the sales force need to call on these accounts this often? Could they
  be redeployed elsewhere to better effect?

Heinz had lost ground in the cooperative sector to other brands and to own
label. When they stopped calling on all Tesco stores (at Tesco's instigation),
they diverted some of the savings to the co-op societies, and regained their
losses (it may also have been that competitors were neglecting co-ops,
leaving an opportunity for Heinz or anyone else). A good costing system
would allow them to judge the extent to which such a switch of resources
was worthwhile.

- Do we have to sell all our brands and varieties in every channel?
- If some outlets restrict the products they will accept, which ones
  should we supply? This applies particularly where space limitations
  conflict with broad ranges (which means in most categories these
  days).

The evidence suggests that activity-related costs which support the
relationship with the customer can account for up to 60 per cent of sales
value, and that these costs can vary widely between customers. (For this
and a more detailed discussion, see the article by Bellis-Jones listed in the
reading list at the end of the chapter.)

This leads naturally to direct product profitability. This was discussed
earlier (in Chapter 5). Whatever the usefulness (or lack of it) in relation to
customers, its logic ought to be applied to the manufacturer's own

operations. It is simply good management practice to know what it costs for the whole chain of activities from production to delivery, and to try to optimize these. It should perhaps be repeated that all costs cannot be minimized without sub-optimizing, because of the trade-offs between different activities (minimizing stock-holding costs may mean a lower level of customer service and greater probability of stock-outs, for example).

New and currently fashionable concepts such as just-in-time delivery, and time-based competition are throwing light on to some of these hitherto neglected areas of cost (see Chapter 8 for further discussion of these ideas). From the point of view of this book, the relationship with customers must remain the focus. What can we do better or cheaper? How can we help our customers? How can we use information to sell to our customers? What data will our customers and competitors be using? One major retailer, on telling one of its suppliers that it was moving from store delivery to central warehousing, insisted on receiving the 4 per cent of turnover which the manufacturer would save, because 'we know that's what it costs you'. What does the average national account manager reply to that?

Budgets and reports

Much of managers' lives revolve around the periodic budget reports they receive (daily, weekly, monthly etc). The important thing to insist on is that once again you receive the information you need when you need it, and in the format which is most helpful.

A colleague has built up a worldwide consultancy business supplying relatively simple software packages to marketing and sales managements of large, sophisticated multinational manufacturers. The software presents forecasts and budget and sales data in the format which managers want, and in a user-friendly way. The large and expensive central computer and accounting departments had apparently not been able to provide these.

The exact nature and format of the report each manager needs will obviously vary considerably. The system should allow each user to receive or call up analyses by customer as well as brand. Year-on-year comparison and performance against target are normally valuable (though surprisingly not always available). Graphic representations can help understanding, and are often fairly easy with current software.

The points made above about the cost of information, and the rules for selection, apply here too. On-line systems can avoid the situation often seen in the early days of computer reporting, when managers disappeared under stacks of print-out; but holding large databases in disaggregated form gets expensive.

Sales forecasting

Although this could be treated as marketing rather than accounting information, it is included here as it is bound up with budgets and reporting. From this book's viewpoint, stress should again be laid on customers, rather than on the intricacies of techniques.

As one trade marketing exponent put it, 'At the moment we are reactive: if we notice that we're losing facings or SKUs in Sainsbury's, we produce data to try to counteract that. What we should be doing is to forecast the impact on our sales of the fact that Tesco is increasing its overall market share.'

Sales forecasting is curiously neglected in many marketing departments. It will become more important in those firms adopting a time-based approach, but it may not be done by marketing people. This reflects the changing role of the marketing function; this important topic is returned to in Chapter 8.

Production information

Much of the information we need on production will be produced by the accounting system already discussed. In particular, detailed data on costs will be extremely important.

As mentioned in an earlier chapter, the focus on customers and the adoption of DPP has often thrown new light on what marketing people need to know about manufacturing. Taking a customer-focused approach to total profitability demands a real understanding of the firm's production processes. If you don't even know that the factory produces three sizes at the same time, how can you make sensible decisions about DPP, optimal order sizes, and discount structures?

The information needed is therefore both quantitative and qualitative. Marketing people need to have a firm grasp of the cost–volume–profit relationships involved in their production processes, and the understanding needs to be based on real, reliable data. They also need to know enough about the production department's goals, culture and constraints that they do not make unjustifiable assumptions about what is feasible and desirable.

The more that packaging and logistics become part of the negotiations between manufacturers and retailers, the more do sales and marketing people need to have at their fingertips the knowledge of how their production system can respond. Retailers are likely to ask for such things as mixed cases or pallets, or trays which fit their shelf configuration, as well as specific delivery volumes and times. The well-prepared account manager will have foreseen these demands and will have the necessary information on whether the request can be met, and on whether it is profitable to meet it. One of the major complaints by retailers against the manufacturers' representatives who deal with them is that the person negotiating does not have the authority to make decisions. Often this can be due to ignorance; that position is no longer tenable. This stance has implications, of course, for organizational structure and lines of authority. Chapter 8 will argue that in fact the national account manager needs greater authority in order to do the job that needs to be done.

External

The unique contribution of marketing as a function is to focus its attention outside the business – on markets, buyers, competitors and the changing environment. Any manufacturer worth its salt ought to know everything there is to know about its markets. Retailers recognize this, and welcome the contribution that the manufacturer can make in passing on some of this information and understanding. This is a major strength and should be capitalized on. However sophisticated retailers become, and however much market research they carry out or buy, they can never know as much about every one of the product markets in which they deal as the manufacturers.

Let us then look at the sort of information we need – on markets, consumers, retailers and competitors.

Market information

To repeat, the manufacturer should know all that is to be known about his or her markets (always allowing for the rules on information set out above). Most consumer goods manufacturers routinely collect data on market size, structure, brand shares etc., broken down by region, channel and so on. There is little need to elaborate on this here, except for some general comments.

First, manufacturers seem curiously unable or unwilling to look at markets from the consumers' point of view. They define markets – and therefore brand shares and market dynamics – in terms of products, for example 'count lines' in confectionery. Do you think that consumers think of the market as limited to count lines when they are choosing a brand? In some markets, of course, product-bound definitions are appropriate (washing powder, shampoo), though even here manufacturers are prone to look at product segments which may be far less clear-cut in consumers' minds than in theirs. In other markets such as snacks, or some durables, consumers may be looking across a range of product fields when deciding how to spend their money. Concentrating only on one's own narrow sector may be misleading. You may be holding share of your narrowly-defined market, for example, but that market may be losing ground to an allied one in which you are not represented, or are less strong.

This leads on to the second remark, that manufacturers need to see accurately what trends are going to affect the market. Factors which may affect demand include demographic and social changes, economic trends, governmental and supra-governmental policies (European Communities legislation, GATT agreements and so on) as well as technological change. Manufacturers must look broadly as well as deeply in trying to anticipate future needs. Most really traumatic changes come from outside existing markets, and manufacturers who do not take a broad view can be caught napping (as Swiss watchmakers were by electronic watches, for example).

Finally, there is the issue of actually using the market data which one has. My impression is that many companies have cupboards (or, these days, computer memories) full of data that no one ever looks at. The pressures of the moment are so compelling that there is simply no time to devote to the detailed analysis which could reveal so much. Marketing and sales departments have no past history, only memories and folk myths. No one has had the time (and the skills) to carry out the rigorous analysis which might lead to real understanding. There is so little that we really know in marketing, know in the sense of having generalizable laws and models which actually work more than once, that the neglect of all this past data seems tremendously wasteful. The rapid turnover of young managers does not help. Perhaps a new sort of person is needed, an archivist-analyst who can distil and preserve what is valuable for future use from the huge mass of numbers which pass through our hands. Better-trained, less computer-phobic marketing and sales people will also help, of course.

Consumer information

As with market data, manufacturers routinely collect information on consumers. If a marketing department does anything at all, it should provide understanding of consumers. Again, there is little to add to what is already well known. Three points bear repetition and underlining about the sort of information which is crucially important.

The first is that what we need to understand is the product in use. Much market research tells us a lot about who consumers are, where they shop, what they buy, what their attitudes and preferences are, what advertising they remember and so on. None of this is unimportant, but it is less vital than something which is not always measured – where the product fits into consumers' lives, what their goals are, what they are trying to achieve when they use the product, what problems occur, what alternatives are considered. . .? American Indians have a saying that you should not judge a man until you have walked two months in his moccasins; perhaps marketing people should try it.

Brand managers can be heard saying casually (and rather patronizingly), things like, 'Of course, housewives always underdose' (that is, use less of the product than is recommended by the manufacturer). Why do housewives do that? Might the brand manager not draw some conclusion from the fact that what most users actually do is not what they 'ought' to do?

On the other hand, a Japanese manufacturer of domestic electronic products recently conducted a very detailed study of how consumers use their durables. A senior manager (Japanese) from the UK subsidiary accompanied a researcher on a two- or three-hour visit to a small number of homes drawn from a tightly defined target market. They studied exactly where each appliance was in the house, and how it was used, when, for what purposes. Such an exercise, though qualitative, must have given them much greater insight into their consumers' wants and needs than standard ratings of brand attributes.

Companies must think carefully exactly what information they need about consumers, so that they can understand the product in use.

The second point is that we must understand the brand. The point has been made before, but cannot be overemphasized, that building and sustaining strong brands is the central task of the marketing department. Research is therefore needed which contributes to an understanding of exactly what the particular brand is, what makes it a brand and not just a product. By definition this must include the name, packaging, price, advertising, and the particular mix of attributes or benefits. Much research effort is devoted to these aspects, and there is no simple, cheap way of guaranteeing useful results. If manufacturers' brands are to survive, however, and are to be the base for future profits, then it is worth spending time and money on the right information.

The third point is that we need to understand consumer shopping habits and preferences in relation to our brands. Again, quantitative data on who shops where, how often, and so on, are readily available. But beyond that we know relatively little about the dynamics of shopping. A multi-buy promotion may produce an effect ten times greater in Tesco than in Sainsbury's for a particular brand; but at present we really do not know why. Shopping, even for low-involvement packaged goods, may be a more complex process than we imagined – but we need to understand it. This may be an area for joint activity with customers, since both would benefit, though clearly real trust would have to exist between the partners.

Information on customers

Chapter 3 discussed in some detail the process of knowing your customers. Here we merely summarize what information should be collected to underpin that process.

General information on retailing

It is important to keep an eye on developments at a general level, since these may change the way you do business – by opening up new outlets, for example, or closing down existing ones. Information should be collected on:

- *External trends*: changes (demographic, socioeconomic etc.) which will affect buying patterns in your customers' markets.
- *Changes affecting the retail business*: technological or legal changes such as tele-shopping or Sunday opening.
- *Changes in distribution channels*: changing transport systems or costs, new forms of competition, encroachment from other sectors; developments in other countries, especially lead countries such as USA, western Europe or, increasingly, Japan.
- *Competitive structure*: current and likely future trends in competition such as discounting or increased specialization.

Information on each customer

There should be a dossier on each of your major customers, containing all the intelligence that can be gathered. Sources will include published information and subjective reporting from the sales force and indeed all parts of your company. The following gives an indication of the range.

- *Financial*: basic data from published accounts are available either direct from the companies or in summary form from one of the many databases such as Extel or DataStream. From these can be calculated financial ratios such as profitability to sales, return on capital employed and so on. These are useful in themselves, but become more meaningful when compared with others in the sector. Comparisons with your own firm's financial performance may be instructive, but should probably not be used in negotiation. The stock market price is increasingly important in this age of acquisition; reports published by stockbrokers contain analyses and comment which vary considerably in quality, but are worth scanning.
- *Market share*: retailers, like manufacturers, now look anxiously at their market shares. Total volume and value shares are useful, particularly if they can be used to set a customer's share of your own market against their overall share.
- *Strategy*: intelligence from trade journals, interviews, speeches, conferences, as well as reports from face-to-face meetings, all contribute to the building up of a picture of the future direction of effort. Like military intelligence, the information needs careful evaluation to sort out reality from fantasy or deliberate disinformation. Of particular interest are target markets and segments, positioning, and the policies that flow from those decisions.
- *Merchandising policy*: of specific interest is the set of decisions on what products to stock and how to display and promote them, within the context of the retailer's strategy; what is the merchandising policy trying to achieve (apart from profit)?
- *Retailer's brands*: this is clearly a key factor, and needs to be monitored closely.
- *Your brands in their market*: the relationship of your brands to your customer's business will affect the nature of the relationship. Is the product field large or small, traffic-builder or peripheral, KVI (known value item) or price-insensitive etc?
- *Direct product profitability*: how do your brands stack up within the total range?

- *Physical distribution*: again, trade journals and personal contacts will provide information not only on current policies, but on likely future changes.
- *Electronic point of sale and scanning*: the potential effects of this have been stressed, and the way the data will be used needs to be watched carefully.
- *People*: all companies are influenced by the people who run them. The successful retailers have often been built up by strong personalities – John Sainsbury, George Davies of Next, Ralph Halpern of Burton Group, Terence Conran of Habitat. It is important to understand these individuals and their likely impact, but it is also vital to know and understand those who put the grand strategy into effect. Knowing the people is as important as reading the published statements.
- *Decision processes*: it follows that you must know for each customer two things about their decision processes – the official policy, and who is actually important in each type of decision. Retailers complain if manufacturers try to bypass well-established procedures, and rightly so; protocol is important. In some companies, however, there are informal routes as well as formal ones.

All these types of information are important, but there is still one major area left out. The application of marketing principles ought to lead us there. These are our customers, and we ought to know:

- What do they want from us?
- What do they think of us?

Manufacturers spend large sums on market research on consumers; how many spend anything at all on researching their customers in the same way? Objective information is essential, and this cannot be obtained through normal personal contacts. Sometimes this sort of information can provide invaluable, though not comfortable, insights, as the following extracts from a syndicated report from the UK show (*Mintel Special Report – Trade Marketing* 1989).

Buyers see problems with inexperienced NAMs (national account managers) who make poor presentations and have no authority to negotiate.

The standard of presentations is. . .not perceived as being particularly high. Reasons given are: overlong; excessive bias in favour of manufacturers; repetitious; inexperienced and poorly trained presenters; ignoring retailers' operational limitations.

Retailers praised United Biscuits for its all-round professionalism and in particular the time they devote to major accounts.

High-quality marketing information and analysis are the main reasons for other companies being praised.

These sorts of inputs can lead directly to action, which will in turn improve the effectiveness of a company's marketing effort. Perhaps as important, they may correct misapprehension as to the real situation. You may think you have an excellent sales operation, but what do your customers think? Trade research, both regular standard surveys and ad hoc studies in relation to, for example, new brand launches, are now much more common. Market research firms specialize in the area, and many large agencies have at least a division with expertise.

Finally, perhaps crucially, see yourself as your customer sees you. What do your brands give them, in terms of profit, store traffic, excitement, contribution to their strategic development? Try summarizing what your major customers would say about you on all the relevant dimensions:

- volumes and margins generated;
- customer service level (percentage of orders/deliveries correct etc., measured in their terms);
- quality of people;
- other aspects of the relationship (flexibility, willingness to respond to customer demands, etc.);
- total brand quality;
- new product development record;
- overall status as preferred supplier. Of course, it would make sense to check with customers what exactly are their relevant criteria for judging you.

Competitor intelligence

Some commentators have argued that companies should concentrate not on consumers, but rather on competitors (notably Ries and Trout in their pithy and entertaining *Marketing Warfare*). This seems to me to go too far; the major focus of marketing must be the consumer. The exaggeration does however contain a major truth. In today's crowded markets, positioning the brand against competition, finding the sustainable competitive advantage, defending your position against attack, are all important strategic considerations. We can certainly never ignore or underestimate competitors, and the increasing internationalization of many markets means that new competitors will be arriving.

As in war, intelligence on the enemy's intentions, strength, disposition and movements is vital input to both strategic and tactical decisions. Most firms have one or two major competitors who dominate and lead their particular markets; detailed information will be collected on these. How detailed will depend to some extent on resources, but large firms spend considerable amounts on finding out about their rivals.

A marketing manager working for a British multinational was sitting on a transatlantic flight, and got out some papers relating to some private insurance he was considering. His neighbour, satisfied that he was not in the same business, got out his files and also started to work. The British manager found out, by reading surreptitiously, that his neighbour worked for the main US competitor and that the file contained personality profiles of the senior managers of the British company. The US rival thought it worth going to the trouble of finding out about individual managers in the competition, presumably so that they could more accurately forecast what they would do in certain circumstances.

This seems extreme, but the role of competitor intelligence should be to try to ensure that you are never caught by surprise by your rivals' moves, and that you can predict accurately how they will react to what you do.

Much of the information of value will be available within the marketplace, and much will be gathered routinely. As with data on customers, it is a matter of making sure that all the snippets are actually collected, and that someone has the job of interpreting them and circulating the results.

In principle, you should aim to know almost as much about competitors as about your own operations. Overall goals, strategies, policies, target segments, positioning, production costs, discount structures, sales force organization, reputation in the trade, calibre of managers. . .all these and more should be covered by the intelligence system. The SWOT (strengths, weaknesses, opportunities, training) analysis again provides a useful framework, but needs considerable filling in in detail.

For the purposes of this book, of course, we are interested specifically in those aspects of the operation which impinge on customers. Policies and organization will be of particular value, and need to be monitored for possible developments. Often the retailers try to play one supplier off against the others, and claims as to what each manufacturer is prepared to offer are the small change of negotiation. As with other information, careful evaluation is needed.

Storing, retrieving and disseminating the information

It was said earlier that the technology used in information storage and retrieval is less important than the thinking that goes into the design of the system. Ideally, it would be sensible to store all the data in a computer system so that whoever needs any of it can retrieve it at will. This may be possible, though for some smaller firms it may not be economic.

What surely is vital is that someone must have the responsibility of ensuring that that system is set up and that it runs, i.e. that reports are collected and filed, that sales call reports are copied to the relevant dossier and so on. This leads directly to the question of organization, which is dealt with in Chapter 8.

Summary

To work effectively with customers it is important to bring to bear a mass of information from different sources. A market and customer information system has the potential to offer real strategic advantage. To commit resources to its development must therefore be an informed board decision.

Although cheaper computer power means that at least part of the system will be computer-based, it is the quality of thinking and planning that goes into the design of the system that is most important.

The categories of information to be assembled are:

Internal
- Accounting
  Product profitability
  Customer profitability
  Budgets and reports
  Sales forecasts

- Production

External
- Markets
- Consumers
- Customers
- Competitors

Top management, and sales and marketing people, must be familiar with the assumptions underlying accounting data. Many conventional accounting systems produce cost and profit figures which may be seriously misleading. Activity analysis should be used.

Since collecting and storing data cost money, some rules of thumb should be applied in deciding what to collect:

- What decisions will we need to make, and what information will be needed to help those decisions?
- What would we do differently if we had that information?
- How would we use it in working with customers?
- What information are our competitors using, and what advantage do they gain from it?

Customer profitability may be a new focus for many manufacturers. They should use the new information to answer such questions as:

- What exactly are we getting out of this combination of brands and customers?
- Do sales people need to call on this customer this often, or could some of their time be usefully redeployed?
- Should we try to sell all varieties of all our brands in all outlets, or would some sub-set be more profitable?
- If some customers restrict the number of SKUs, which particular combination would be most profitable for us?

  Overall, try to see yourself as your customers see you. Summarize their view of you in terms of volumes and margins generated, customer service level, quality of people, other aspects of the relationship, total brand quality, new product development record, and status as preferred supplier.

Further reading

Bellis-Jones, Robin (1989), 'Customer profitability analysis', *Management Accounting*, February.

Enis, Ben M. and Broome, C. L. (1973), *Marketing Decisions: A Bayesian Approach*, Aylesbury: Intertext.

FitzRoy, Peter T. (1976), *Analytical Methods for Marketing Management*, Maidenhead: McGraw Hill.

Johnson, Thomas H. and Kaplan, R. (1987), *Relevance Lost: The Rise and Fall of Management Accounting*, Harvard: Harvard Business School Press.

Ries, A. and Trout, J. (1982), *Positioning*, New York: McGraw Hill.

Ries, A. and Trout, J. (1986), *Marketing Warfare*, New York: McGraw Hill.

Ries, A. and Trout, J. (1989), *Bottom-up Marketing*, New York: McGraw Hill.

7
Implanting customer thinking

Chapter 1 demonstrated that there has been a profound change in the relationship between consumer goods manufacturers and the retailers whom they supply. Retail concentration and the growth of multiples has changed the balance of power. Retail managers have become very much more sophisticated, and buying is generally more centralized. Manufacturers who do not recognize this and adapt to it will suffer profoundly. Those who do stand to gain a significant competitive advantage.

It has been a long and sometimes painful struggle for many manufacturers to adopt a marketing viewpoint, in the sense of making the consumer the focus of the company's thinking. Now they are being asked to change again, and think about customers. In reality there is no difference. I have argued that focusing on customers is simply applying basic marketing principles, but adding a new group of people as the target of our marketing effort.

The fact is that this apparently simple change raises enormous psychological barriers in some people and companies. I have quoted the examples of feelings approaching paranoia shown at times by some manufacturers. Not only are the changes unpleasant, in the sense of introducing new and unwelcome pressures into the day-to-day job – they are threatening to a whole way of thinking and acting.

It is well known that individuals react differently to such threatening changes, though all pass through the same stages.

One model of reactions to change shows seven such stages:

- Immobilization
- Minimization
- Depression
- Acceptance of reality – letting go
- Testing
- Search for meaning
- Internalization

At present, managers in manufacturing companies can be observed at all these stages. There are certainly some still at the immobilization stage – the rabbit in the headlights syndrome. Such people deny the existence of significant change, and carry on as they have done for years. Most seem to move quite quickly to the second stage, that of accepting that something has indeed changed but denying that it is important. Senior Sales Directors – and surprisingly even some retailers – can be found saying that really the situation does not demand radical new approaches to business, merely minor adaptations. Even manufacturers who recognize and complain vociferously about the power of multiples treat it as something 'out there' and nothing they themselves can do anything about. Trade marketing is regarded with suspicion, as just an excuse for giving more money to the retailers. In the depressed phase, too, little action is seen. All these first three stages involve a paralysis of the managerial will; the company will do little or nothing to adapt to the changes which are transforming its world.

Manufacturers must break out of this deadening phase, and like all organizational changes this must be led from the top. The difficulties must be recognized and not minimized. A great many people at all levels of the firm are going to be asked to give up ways of thinking and acting that are second nature to them – indeed which have been the foundation of their business success so far. To change all these people will take time and effort. Two examples from Procter and Gamble, generally recognized as one of the best companies in this as well as other fields, are revealing.

In the USA, Procter and Gamble has for many years been recognized as a formidably effective marketer of consumer goods. Its relationship with retailers was, however, one of respect rather than affection: retailers felt that the company told them what they would accept and when, with no consultation. (Incidentally, this gave a competitive opportunity to Lever Brothers, as retailers were happy to help them try to build share against

Procter.) At top management level, Procter was one of the first to recognize that they needed to change, and the company made a public commitment to work with customers rather than against them. This has now been official policy for some time. As one East Coast retailer said, however, 'This doesn't seem to have reached the field reps yet: they still come in just as they always have and tell us what shipments of which brands and sizes we're going to get.'

In the UK, P and G have also adopted the working with customers approach. As a symbol, they decided to give up using the phrase 'the trade', which was seen to have patronizing overtones too reminiscent of the bad old days; instead, all references will be to 'customers'. Spend some time with Procter people, even those who are leading the process of change, and you will still hear 'the trade' creeping into conversation. It is very hard to break the habits of a lifetime. The example is important because habits of speech reflect habits of thinking. The reorientation has to permeate everyone's thinking, deep into the company, and this does not happen overnight. (It should be stressed that Procter and Gamble have none-the-less made more progress towards real customer orientation than most other firms; in this, as in other areas, they set the standards.)

To change the corporate culture, then, takes determination from the top, and detailed planning and follow-up. Statements of policy are not enough. The detailed implications of the new approach need to be thought through for all departments, and changes made at all levels. Education and training will be necessary, and even salary packages may need to reflect the new priorities. Organizational changes will certainly be needed, and are dealt with in Chapter 8.

One factor which has been inhibiting rapid adaptation in many companies is organizational politics, and in particular the rivalry or mistrust which unfortunately still prevails between sales and marketing. The customer viewpoint, or trade marketing, can become the victim of such dysfunctional stresses; it is extremely important to get top management support, and to design the appropriate structure, as discussed in the next chapter.

Pinpointing resistance

As Machiavelli's famous quotation reminds us, 'There is nothing more difficult to arrange, more doubtful of success, and more dangerous to carry through than initiating changes' to an established system. It is important to recognize at the outset that many people will resist. They must be identified and their concerns addressed if effective action is to be taken. Experienced managers know that a new way of doing things needs to be carefully and sometimes forcefully sold to a great many people if it is to be adopted thoroughly. The stage that must be reached is the internalization by all concerned of the new policy.

Resistance will be encountered at all levels, from the top to the bottom. In one major multinational, the corporate manager responsible for driving through a radical reorientation towards customers has identified some chairmen of subsidiary companies who are resistant. His view is that the desired changes will not happen unless and until these very senior managers are removed: they are too old or too set in their ways to change, and it is they who must lead the spread of the new policies in their companies.

If this is an extreme situation, there are more common points of likely resistance.

Marketing

In many successful consumer-goods companies the marketing department has, often after a long struggle, established itself as central to strategy and operations. The marketing people know about consumers, and therefore must control or have a very important input to decisions about products, packaging, pricing, advertising and promotion – indeed most of the major decisions the firm must make. Focusing on customers as well as on consumers challenges this marketing hegemony. As we shall see, a new orientation may demand organizational changes which appear to diminish substantially marketing's influence. At the very least, new tensions will be set up between the demands of consumers as backed by the marketing department and other priorities of customer needs and the overall desire to optimize the company's share of the profits available in the value chain which stretches from raw materials through production and distribution to final purchase and consumption. The jealousy and rivalry between marketing and sales, mentioned above, are likely to be exacerbated rather than soothed by the perceived threat of loss of power.

Sales force

The sales force will have already seen most changes. Many of the old, large sales teams of several hundred field representatives, with area managers, regional managers and so on, are no more. National account groups are now common, telephone sales teams have replaced the reps calling on all stores, and the total size of the sales department is likely to be less than 100. More radical change is needed, however, and as the Procter and Gamble example showed, may be more difficult to achieve. Although not entirely related to age, resistance may be expected especially among older (and often therefore more senior) members of the sales team. This results not only from the change in the balance of power, but from the nature of the job that the sales person is expected to do. The impact of new technology is particularly relevant. Anyone negotiating with retailers must be conversant with the implications of scanning, computerized stock control and ordering, space management and direct product profitability, computer-controlled direct store delivery and so on; successful companies will be ahead of the game in understanding new developments and seeking to profit from them. Many sales people, particularly older ones, suffer from technophobia, and have to be dragged kicking and screaming to a personal computer. They will become an increasing problem as buyers continue to become more sophisticated. While the personal relationships will remain important, and while much negotiation will continue to revolve around price and margin, the old skills and qualities will no longer be enough. Sales people who cannot adapt will have to be found roles where they can still contribute, or be retired. In one case, the retailer has actually suggested to the managing director of a major manufacturer that a particular (older) national account manager be retired and the young, marketing-trained account manager be left to carry on the excellent job he is doing. The new attitudes and skills needed to deal successfully with customers are so different from the traditional ones – and so central to the relationship – that hard decisions will have to be made.

Manufacturing

Production managers have traditionally complained that the demands of the marketing department make their life impossible, but now they may find another set of requirements. Not only will retailers want just-in-time deliveries, they may also demand special packs or variants, particular sets of assortments (size, flavour etc.), and outers/pallets which fit their shelves. Coming on top of drives from top management for increases in efficiency, rationalization of plants and introduction of new technology, these changes will be resisted by manufacturing.

Physical distribution

For a long time physical distribution has been the Cinderella, a low-level, mechanical operation to which marketing and sales people paid little attention. Pressures from customers, and from within the firm itself, have changed that. Delivery is now part of the marketing mix targeted at customers, but while physical distribution managers may welcome the new prominence which this gives them and their department, they will also face conflict between customers' demands and the company's search for increased efficiency. Scheduling will be more complex, and the managers involved will need new skills – quantitative, computing and personal skills such as negotiation. People wedded to the good old days will find ways of resisting change.

Accounting and finance

The accounts department will also face change from within and from outside. From the customers' point of view, trade terms, ordering and payment systems are now negotiable; marketing and sales teams will want to 'interfere' in matters previously the concern of the accountant. They will also want different sorts of information from that which the accounts department have traditionally provided – costs and profitability by customer, for example.

In all these cases (and there are probably more rather than fewer points of resistance), the changes may not appear great, and the possible resistance to them may seem childish and futile. Be that as it may, people do resist change. The company's planning must take this into account, so that objections can be brought into the open and dealt with. Examples of major changes in company culture, such as British Airways' retraining of most of its huge staff in order to make them more sensitive to customers' needs, show what can be achieved, but also what a massive effort is needed. Half-hearted attempts will fail, given the normal inertia built into every organization. As Kenichi Ohmae has written (*Harvard Business Review*, Jan–Feb 1989):

> ...The critical issue is the mind-set of managers, their willingness to look at their businesses and their customers' needs with continually fresh eyes. More than their willingness – their insistence. It is human nature to resist change, to stick with what you've got, to do more of what you know how to do well. But that only makes it more important for managers consciously

to refuse to take their business systems or their definitions of customer values as givens. It is their high responsibility to rethink those business systems on a regular basis, to take them apart in their minds, to go through a disciplined mental process of decomposing them and then restructuring them from scratch, from a zero-based foundation.

How deep into the organization?

It is an oversimplification to say that the traditional pattern of manufacturer–retailer relationship consisted of sales people calling on buyers and store managers, but it is worth exaggerating to focus attention on how dramatically the situation has changed. It is a revealing exercise to try to think how many people in your customer's organization you ought to be in contact with. How many do you think – five? ten? twenty? Procter and Gamble conducted a detailed study of one of their biggest customers: they identified fifty people with whom they wished to have contacts.

This may be something of a shock at first, but it follows logically from the need to understand your customer thoroughly. Obviously the main contacts will continue to be buyers, but there are more of them now: more buying groups per retailer, and more staff in each buying group. Some buying groups contain their own marketing specialists, and there are often separate merchandising, pricing and new product groups or committees. Beyond that, you need to understand how their information systems work and how they are developing, exactly how they deal with the handling of goods in the store and in their warehouses, and so on. Virtually every aspect of the retailer's operations is of concern, and your aim should be to understand his or her total business better than any one of his or her own staff.

Having identified with whom in the customer you need to be in contact, you can decide who in your company should take responsibility for each target. The nature of the relationship and the frequency of contact will vary, but it should be clear that customer thinking must penetrate deep into the company. Everything you do which might affect customers must be reconsidered with them in mind, and against the criteria, 'How can we make it easier for the customer to buy our products, how can we help them to improve their business?' Everything from the ordering system through design of invoices, the computer operating systems and communication protocols, the way the telephone is answered, pack design, traded unit packaging, assortment of varieties in outers or on pallets to delivery schedules and payment systems will be involved. Bob Townsend, in his famous book *Up the Organisation*, said that everyone in the firm is the marketing department, and that thinking applies to working with customers. It is not just the concern of sales and marketing people, or of a few new staff labelled 'trade marketing', but of everyone.

Just who in your company will be allowed to speak to whom in your customers' will of course depend on their willingness to cooperate. Some retailers are much more open than others. Ideally, your PDM people should be visiting the retailers' warehouses, your systems experts talking to theirs, your accountants consulting their opposite numbers, right through the range of activities which make up the totality of the relationship. Some of these contacts may be occasional telephone calls, others will involve more frequent and more formal meetings or joint working groups, while still others may be social in context.

Social mixing seems common at the higher levels of management, with dinners, golf matches and the gamut of business entertaining giving opportunities for senior managers and directors to mingle and get to know each other. Conferences, too, are good places to meet customers away from the sometimes tense arena of negotiation. Currently, my impression is that these contacts do not spread very far down the organizations. It follows from the argument above that social as well as business mixing across a very wide front could be beneficial. We must never forget that the relationships are made up of people. It is not necessary that all the participants love each other, but basic human contact normally makes it easier to do business with someone – being able to put a face to a name or a voice on the telephone.

It is fair to say that there may be resistance to attempts at social mixing, especially if it appears as mere supplier entertaining which is aimed too overtly at buying favours, or at providing opportunities for wheedling information out of buyers. Female staff in particular were found in one study to be suspicious of entertaining by manufacturers, and generally against any social mixing outside working hours (and the number of women managers will certainly increase). Occasions should be carefully targeted to appeal to the variety of retailer staff you wish to involve. Those who are open to entertainment like to attend free major sports events; some more seriously minded people will only go for factory visits or educational events. Non-threatening occasions which encourage participation, such as ten-pin bowling evenings, can be attractive.

The other negative point which must be made is that some retailers such as Marks and Spencer actually discourage the formation of any relationship at all between suppliers' representatives and their buyers. To that end, buyers are rotated about every eighteen months so that no relationship can be formed. This is not to prevent corruption, but is based on the belief that the buyer must remain objective at all times; that objectivity might be compromised by even a superficial social relationship.

None of this is to suggest that the relationship between a manufacturer and a retailer will ever be one of total openness and complete cooperation. They are always competing to some extent for the total profit available, and their objectives will sometimes conflict. The manufacturer will not want to reveal all his or her plans, and neither will the retailer. Having said that, it must be true that more knowledge of each other, more openness, more contacts across a wide front, will all contribute to the recognition that the two parties really do have a common interest in working together in satisfying consumers. The better the relationship, the more trust that has been built up, the easier it will be to solve the really difficult issues which will inevitably arise.

Nor is it the purpose to suggest that manufacturers should aim to meet all the needs and wishes of retailers, or to give up their control of their marketing activity – indeed exactly the opposite. The whole point of working with customers is that it is designed to keep control by anticipating and meeting their needs in a way which meets your own objectives and guarantees your continuing profitability. Without this pro-active attitude there is a real danger that retailer power and sophistication will take control of the relationship and erode your profit margin at the expense of theirs.

Customer thinking – the augmented product

The analogy between marketing to retail customers and industrial marketing has already been made – the need to manage a long-term relationship with a fairly small number of large clients is common to both. One of the best definitions of marketing was given in an industrial context by the Chairman of Carborundum in the USA. The company had a long-standing reputation for making grinding wheels, but as the Chairman put it, 'Our customers don't want grinding wheels, they want metal removed.' This change in thinking led Carborundum to learn much more about their customers' businesses, what tasks they were undertaking, what objectives they were seeking to fulfil, what problems they had – and then to look for ways in which Carborundum could help them. This led to a range of products and services – including but not confined to grinding wheels – which fitted customers' needs.

This approach has been christened the augmented product. It means thinking about what the customer wants to buy rather than merely what we happen to want to sell. It may lead to a package of products and services, often including components previously outside the seller's product range, which offer the customer real benefits. IBM was a conspicuously successful practitioner of such an approach for many years (though it has mainly sold only products it manufactured itself).

Customer thinking which pervades the consumer-goods manufacturer will produce a similar approach. Inclusion of products or components from other manufacturers is less likely than in industrial marketing, perhaps (though not impossible). More likely are new ways of ordering or delivery and added information. Some examples were given earlier; here are some more ways of adding to the bare product offering things which will give real benefits to the retailer:

- Shrink-wrapping packs on trays to cut down handling time.
- Shrink-wrapping sub-units within the tray (fours, sixes etc.) to match facings requirements.
- Mixing varieties within the traded unit to match the sales pattern of the customer's outlets (six regular, three orange, two lemon, one lime, for example).
- Altering the size of outers or traded units to fit the customer's shelf.
- Working jointly on a just-in-time delivery schedule.
- Carrying out direct product profitability studies and space management analyses; advising on maximizing a category's potential.
- Providing information on the whole market, on trends in consumer tastes and lifestyles.
- Working jointly on ordering procedures, leading to automatic electronic reordering.

The overriding need is to look afresh at all your ways of doing business. Apparently the favourite words of Konosuke Matsushita (founder of the world-leading Matsushita Electric Industrial) were: *Torawenai sunao-na kokoro* which means 'Mind that does not stick'. Minds must not be allowed to stick on old ways of operating, or to obstruct new ways of thinking. Everyone must search restlessly for the new opportunities opening up.

Summary

Adopting a customer focus may sound simple, but it involves profound changes in an organization. Individuals faced with threatening change have to pass through phases of immobilization, minimization and depression before they can begin to take positive action.

Change must be led from the top; but even when it is, it takes time to drive new attitudes down through the firm.

It is important to pinpoint likely resistance and forestall it. Most functions will be affected and will resist for their own reasons. Marketing may fear loss of power and influence. Sales people will need new knowledge and skills – computer models and negotiation, for example. Manufacturing and physical distribution will meet fresh demands on them to do things differently. Accountants will be asked for new kinds of information and for new ways of dealing with ordering and invoicing.

The people in target customers with whom you need relationships need to be identified. One manufacturer listed fifty people in one retailer with whom they wished to be in touch. The nature of the relationship with each needs to be defined, and responsibility allocated for contacts and feedback.

In adopting customer thinking, firms should learn from industrial marketers. You must put yourself in customers' shoes and think about their real needs. The concept of the augmented product provides a useful focus. How can what you provide to your customers help them in their business, in terms of the total service – ordering, product design, assortment, packaging, delivery, invoicing and so on?

The overriding need is to look afresh at all the ways you do business. Everyone involved – and that means far more people in your firm than previously – must search restlessly for new approaches to make the most of new opportunities.

Further reading

Bateson, John E. G. (1989), *Managing Services Marketing*, Chicago: The Dryden Press

Plant, Roger (1987), *Managing Change and Making it Stick*, London: Fontana

Townsend, R. (1970), *Up the Organisation*, London: Michael Joseph

Turnbull, Peter and Cunningham, M. T. (1981), *International Marketing and Purchasing*, London: Macmillan

8
Designing the organization

General influences on marketing organization

Before looking in detail at how firms should organize themselves to work more closely with their customers we must look at the overall question of organization design. The reason is that, after a period of relative stability in what was generally accepted as sensible marketing organization, we are entering a time when several pressures, from both within and from outside the firm, are throwing doubt on this accepted wisdom. The three major pressures are:

- The swing in the balance of power to retailers.
- New methods of manufacturing.
- Internationalization.

For many years now, one model – the brand or product manager system – has dominated the marketing organization of fmcg manufacturers. There are other models, and considerable variation in the way that the brand manager model is interpreted, but in general the great majority of manufacturers have a brand manager system. There have always been conceptual and practical problems with the system, in particular the gap between responsibility and authority, but overall it has seemed to make sense to have one person coordinating all the marketing-related activities affecting a brand.

The period from the 1960s through the 1980s during which the brand manager was king (or queen) was also the period which saw the marketing function at the height of its power and influence. An extreme manifestation is the organization chart which shows marketing as the hub of a wheel, with all other functions revolving round it.

This has now changed. The triple pressures from the trade, manufacturing and internationalization have made corporate managers realize that current forms of organization are inadequate. To meet the new challenges, new forms are needed. The problems caused by the new relationship with retailers are the focus of this book, and are returned to later in this chapter. Let us now look briefly at the two other pressures.

New forms of manufacturing

This is shorthand for a new way of looking at the business as a whole, not just the production part of it, although manufacturing is the origin. I am including within the concept a number of developments which combine technological changes with new ways of managing: they are time-based competition (Figure 8.1) (including just-in-time systems), flexible manufacturing systems and the total quality approach.

Efficiencies start in manufacturing, but the approach spreads through the entire organization and out to suppliers and dealers. The lessons are being applied by American companies as well as Japanese, and by service firms as well as manufacturers. From our point of view, the interesting things to emerge concern organization design. Ford's new system puts something called a car program management team at the hub of the wheel; the parts which revolve round this central management include sales and marketing, manufacturing, purchasing etc. The echoes of this will be seen later in this chapter.

It is not within the scope of this book to go into the details of how to go about transforming a firm to time-based competition. One quotation gives the flavour of what is involved (Bower and Hout, *Harvard Business Review*, Nov–Dec 1988):

> Many of these suggestions run counter to traditional ideas about good management. Efficiency was often thought to follow from fixed objectives, clear lines of organization, measures reduced to profit, and as few changes in basic arrangements as possible. But that was the logic of the mass-production machine. It has been superseded by the logic of innovation. And that logic, in turn, demands new organization and management practices.

Time-based competition or fast-cycle capability is a way of arranging the business so as to minimize the time each operation takes. Although this is an old thought ('time is money'), it is being applied by world-class manufacturers with a thoroughness and radicalism which make it new. One particular aspect of this approach is JIT (just-in-time delivery of parts and minimization of inventory), which has received wide publicity. It is only symptomatic of a whole approach, which can have dramatic results.

Best known are the ways in which Japanese manufacturers, especially in the motor car industry, have out-performed their rivals. The figures for Toyota compared with Detroit are revealing:

	Toyota	Detroit
Time taken to develop a new car	3 years	5 years
Cycle time through the plant	2 days	5 days
Time needed to schedule a dealer's order	1 day	5 days
Inventory turns for entire supply chain	16 times/yr	8 times/yr

Old-style manufacturing meant that large buffer stocks of materials, components and work in progress took up expensive space in warehouses and factories. Under JIT most of this is avoided. A simple reordering system named after the Toyota *kanban* (Japanese for shop-sign) has a card attached to the delivery container; this is returned to the supplier, and automatically reorders the goods. The JIT approach has also led to smaller batch sizes, as the old 'economic order quantity' calculations were questioned. This in itself has other spin-offs, particularly in total quality control (see Fig. 8.3 and reading list).

Figure 8.1   Time-based competition

Flexible manufacturing systems have evolved as a result of the information technology revolution. Traditional mass-production systems looked for efficiencies through the economies of scale of long production runs. Making very large quantities of a standard product was the goal; changing to different products involved down-time, and was to be avoided. Although an exaggeration, this description is broadly accurate. The advent of computer-controlled (or computer-integrated) manufacturing has changed this completely. It is said that Ford's Dagenham plant can run without stopping for a year without producing two models exactly the same. IBM's new manufacturing plant can be reprogrammed in 15 minutes to make anything electronic as long as it fits certain maximum dimensions.

Figure 8.2 Flexible manufacturing

What these new systems mean (and of course it should be said that the benefits do not apply equally across all technologies) is that many of the old antagonisms between production and marketing are no longer necessary. Equally, though, the need for close coordination becomes even more important.

Internationalization

There is no question that most industries are becoming more international. The topic is so important that a separate chapter is devoted to it (Chapter 10). What needs to be said here is that traditionally, marketing organization has been designed for one country, taking little or no account of what was happening elsewhere (the only exceptions being countries in which the market was too small to justify an autonomous operation). In many markets, manufacturers have moved rapidly in recent years to thinking internationally, often because of competitive and cost pressures rather than as a result of market needs.

Once the process starts, and senior managers look at a region as one market to be served, decisions are taken above the country level. This has implications for the marketing function just as much as for the others. Although markets are still different, cost pressures may mean that product formulation decisions are taken at regional or global level. Part of

Total quality, like time-based competition, started in manufacturing but has spread to all parts of the organization. Again, Japanese use of quality circles has received most coverage, but the applications are much wider. Many companies in the West are seeking total quality throughout their operations, and are finding that the approach throws up unexpected benefits in efficiency as well as reduction in defects and complaints. Total quality control (TQC) is intimately linked with the time-based approach. The ability to work in smaller batch sizes means that mistakes are noticed much earlier and can be corrected. The individual and team can take a much closer interest in the quality of items produced – and are forced to because the individuals and teams next down the line will notice quickly. This leads to 100 per cent inspection instead of sampling, but also to inspection by the operators themselves rather than by a separate worker. Responsibility is devolved down to individuals and teams, who take a pride in their output and can identify with it. The combination of JIT and TQC leads not only to cost savings through reduced inventory, lower scrap rates and less reworking, but also to higher delivered quality and the ability to respond faster to market needs.

Figure 8.3   Total quality

the marketing function has been taken 'upstairs'. At the very least, the new organization must take account of the needs of harmonization and coordination.

The wonderful inter-relatedness of parts

It is no accident that words such as 'system' and 'coordination' have cropped up so frequently in this discussion. Perhaps the main unifying idea in all these approaches is the inter-relatedness of the different parts of a business. This is of course hardly a revelation, but anyone working in a large organization knows that the different departments do in fact become separated. Specialization is necessary, but can lead to distancing oneself from other departments. Objectives conflict, communication becomes difficult, friction arises, coordination breaks down. The Ford

Motor Company's engineering and manufacturing departments for many years did not have any face to face contact, and spent their time in mutual suspicion and recrimination; it took huge efforts at 'breaking down the chimneys' to eradicate this problem (Pascale 1990).

This seems at least partly a problem of size. Small firms have fewer of these difficulties because it is easier for individuals to see the relationship of their work to that of the firm as a whole. Often separate departments simply do not exist. These lessons are applied to many of these new approaches to managing large firms; small teams take responsibility for whole blocks of work, and manage themselves. It will be interesting to see how far these ideas can be applied to the sales and marketing context.

Specific problems in sales and marketing

The general pressures affecting firms have been described; let us now look at how they impinge on marketing and sales functions. The brand management system was pinpointed above. It was probably never true that the brand manager was 'the managing director of the brand', since few if any have ever had the authority which that implies. Large claims have been made, however, for the scope of the job. The trend in recent years has been to whittle down this scope in many fmcg companies, mainly because firms have finally realized just how important the brands are – certainly too important to be messed around by an arrogant but inexperienced 25-year-old.

It was not long ago that brand managers happily had labels and packaging redesigned at the drop of a hat (some critics felt that that was the main thing they did, just to make an impact before moving on to the next job). Although heavily involved in day-to-day relations with advertising agencies, brand managers have not had a major influence on advertising decisions, whether budget, platform or treatment, for some time. Below-the-line promotions have traditionally been their preserve, and these have come to play a larger and larger part with the siphoning of funds from theme advertising forced by retailer power. The changed nature of the relationship with retailers has meant that more and more of the brand group's activities have been devoted to preparing material for presentations to customers.

There are two major problems produced by these trends:

- Brand managers become mere 'gophers', expensive and hopefully high-quality talent squandered on menial tasks.

- The one unique task of the brand group, to focus on building and maintaining the brand through sensitivity to consumer needs, is neglected; day-to-day pressures mean that the urgent crowds out the important.

The sales force has seen more obvious and more radical changes. Numbers have been dramatically reduced, and the tasks carried out have changed. National account managers and negotiators deal with the major customers, many of whom do not allow sales representatives into the stores. Although personal relationships still matter, and therefore the personal qualities of the sales person are still important, there seems to be little old-fashioned selling to be done (a pardonable exaggeration, as the tasks remain relatively unchanged in some areas such as co-ops and independent grocers, and some trade sectors). Where the job has changed completely, the staff concerned have also had to change, and many have found it hard to adapt.

The obvious problems caused have mainly been mentioned; to summarize, they are:

- Lack of expertise in computer systems, and the new modelling approaches such as direct product profitability (DPP) and space management.
- Lack of knowledge of production and of physical distribution, which are increasingly of interest to customers.
- Poor information-handling and presentation skills.
- Poor negotiation skills.
- Lack of authority to make decisions.

Finally, customers complain of a lack of communication between sales and marketing people. (In one very well-known company the sales people refuse to tell their marketing colleagues what terms are negotiated with retailers, and the marketing staff are similarly close-mouthed with the sales people – hardly a team effort!). While this may always have been true, it is now much more crucial. Taken together, these problems reveal a situation in some firms which needs drastic remedial action. Unfortunately, the political sensitivity and power struggles that seem inherent in the sales–marketing interface in many companies have led firms to shy away from confronting the problem. It is up to top management to address the issue and take decisive action; otherwise, much of what is attempted in improving customer service will remain mere tinkering.

Redesigning the organization – a step-by-step approach

Most fmcg manufacturers have adapted their organizations in some way to the changed environment; the changes vary from the trivial to the profound. What I suggest here is an approach which can be followed through every stage by those who have not yet adapted their structure to work better with customers, and can be used as a checklist by those who have. My research suggests that no firm has yet got everything right.

The steps suggested are:

1 Diagnosis of the situation – where are we now?
   - Company SWOT (strengths, weaknesses, opportunities and training) analysis and strategy development
   - Brand portfolio analysis
   - Diagnosis of retailer situation
   - Sales and marketing SWOT

2 Prognosis – what is likely to happen?
3 Specification of tasks and roles – what needs to be done, and by whom?
4 Examination of options – what are the possible strategies and organizational structures open to us?
5 Selection of best-fit solution – which particular combination suits our situation, culture and resources?
6 Implementation – how do we travel from where we are now to where we want to get to?

These will be examined in turn.

1 Diagnosis of the situation

Company SWOT analysis and strategy development

The trade marketing issue is part of overall corporate strategy. It cannot be tackled in isolation, but must be seen in the context of the firm as a whole. The point was made above that the change in the balance of power between manufacturers and retailers is one of the primary forces demanding a new approach to business, but it is only one. Whatever we decide to do in the sales and marketing area must be tightly tied in with other functional areas; indeed, it may be that the traditional functional departments disappear and that the company adopts a whole new form of organization.

Such changes at corporate level may be radical and quick, or gradual – revolution or evolution. Much will depend on the firm's situation within its specific market: is it a dominant player with large resources, or a minor one whose choices are restricted? Experience of the last few years suggests strongly that an evolutionary approach may be too slow. Time is not on the side of manufacturers, and competitors who move quickly will gain an advantage which will be difficult to counter. Conversely, of course, there is an enormous opportunity for those who have the will and energy to make dramatic strides.

Brand portfolio analysis

Allied to the overall company position is the relative strength of its brand portfolio. This was discussed in Chapter 2, and its importance cannot be overstressed. The current strength of the company's brands, and its commitment to them for the future, form the single most influential factor in deciding its strategy and therefore structure.

The analysis must be objective, and should be based on information on:

● Market share and trend.
● Ratings and preference strength amongst consumers.
● Distribution strength and views of retailers.
● Number, size and strength of competition.
● Production capacity of firm and industry – nationally and internationally.
● Barriers to entry and exit – technological, financial, marketing, strategic.

All lead to the basic question, does this brand have a sustainable competitive advantage?

This and the previous section should also tackle the question of new brand development. Too many corporate plans in the past have relied on optimistic hopes for new brands when the reality of performance is dismal. While it sometimes seems that the worst days of hectic new brand introductions – mostly weak me-too products with no advantage to consumer or trade – are over, in some sectors the failure rate is still unreasonably high. Some manufacturers are clearly focusing on the development of a relatively small number of significant new brands, but others are still rushing in with copies of successful innovations and unjustifiable range extensions. New brand development is a huge and vitally important subject in its own right. All that needs to be said here is that it must be treated carefully and objectively within the context of the firm's strengths and weaknesses, not relied on as a miracle worker.

Diagnosis of retailer situation

Several questions are relevant here. The first is how many trade sectors are involved (that is, different types of outlet). The situations and cultures of different sectors vary substantially, and each needs to be treated separately. A drinks company selling to the on-licence trade (pubs etc.), off-licences and supermarkets has three completely different situations to deal with; each may need different treatment. In principle, the more sectors a manufacturer deals with, the greater its bargaining power, and unfortunately vice versa.

Within each sector we clearly need to look at the structure of the trade in detail, and at the position of our company in each part of it. This is a central part of the analysis; if possible, it should be approached objectively and with fresh eyes. People dealing with customers day in and day out may need to stand back a little, and look at both the recent history and the current situation without prejudice. Questions asked should be both quantitative (what is our share in that sector and that customer, how much of our time and money is spent in achieving these results, what is the competitive situation in each sector and customer?), and qualitative (what is the nature of our relationship with each customer, how do we feel about that part of the business. . .?).

The example was quoted earlier of the cooperative societies apparently being neglected, and therefore offering a competitive opportunity. Other sectors may also be revealed as opportunities to counter the threats so often seen in the major multiples.

Again, objective information (from surveys, for example) on the standing of our company in the trade would be invaluable (and perhaps surprising). What is important to establish is a clear view of where we are starting from now.

Sales and marketing SWOT

The sales and marketing departments are of particular interest in our diagnosis. For the sales force, information is needed on:

- Number, age distribution and quality of sales people.
- Quality of national account managers (NAMs) – age, experience, education, skills (presentation, negotiation, computing), attitudes.
- Number and calibre of support staff.
- Current state of information technology systems.

Equivalent data should be collected on marketing staff, and for both an investigation should be carried out to determine:

- Who is doing what, exactly? Are the brand group spending most of their time on preparing trade presentations? How do the NAMs spend their time? Are all the sectors and accounts receiving their due weight of effort?
- Who holds what information? What information on customers and our relationships with them exists, who has it, who has access to it, who has responsibility for it? What information would we like to have but don't?
- What is the amount and quality of communication between sales and marketing?
- Who actually makes what decisions, and how are they made?
- Who makes decisions on discounts, promotional allowances, special deals? How is planning coordinated?

The point here is to find out what really happens, not just what senior managers think is happening. The larger the organization, the more difficult it is for top management to keep in detailed touch with every part of their empire. The culture of most sales and marketing departments means that they are biased towards activity: the people in them are always busy, or at least give a convincing impression of being busy. Whether they are busy doing the right things is less clear.

2 Prognosis

The term prognosis is borrowed from medical practice: the doctor, having carried out the diagnosis and assessed the current situation, can give an informed view of what is likely to happen. In some fields doctors have a soundly based body of knowledge which allows them to model with confidence the causes which have produced the patient's condition, and also to forecast accurately what will happen from now on. In other fields, as we are all well aware, medical knowledge is less developed, and neither diagnosis nor prognosis can be made with any accuracy or confidence.

Compared with medical science, business and marketing knowledge is primitive. Mainly we rely on individuals' experience and the collective wisdom built up in the company and industry. Market research and other forms of information are available, of course, and in some cases there are quite sophisticated models of daunting mathematical complexity. The more forward-looking firms have been working for twenty years or more on building models through experimentation and measurement, so that they know quite a lot about, for example, advertising–sales relationships and price elasticity. Others, particularly smaller companies, do not even have those.

The real problem, however, is that we are dealing with complexity and change. To forecast what will happen in a system (manufacturer–retailer–consumer systems in this case), we need to have a clear understanding of the causal relationships within the system, and the ability to forecast what will happen to each of the main parameters and variables. Admittedly the formidable complexity of the whole system can be reduced to some extent by concentrating on one or a few market sectors, but this may be a false hope since the retail multiple will be affected by events in other markets apart from ours, and this may in turn affect its actions towards us. In other words, the complexity is aggravated by the interactions between different parts of the overall system.

In dealing with change there is the additional problem of human nature. Because we rely on experience, on what we know from the past and what has worked in the past, we all find it difficult to deal with a future which may be completely different. We have seen that many parts of the manufacturer–retailer system have undergone very radical changes over the last few years. Some manufacturers have not yet fully absorbed these changes, and are not yet responding adequately to them. Others have adapted, but do not necessarily find it easy to go on changing or to foresee the precise shape of things to come.

All this is merely to say that there is a great deal of uncertainty about the future, a fact with which all good business managers are familiar. To say that everything is so complex that we cannot possibly forecast anything is a counsel of despair. Organizations must adapt, and strong firms will want to be proactive, to keep control of their own destiny rather than being swept along with the tide.

One way of dealing with this amount of uncertainty is to use scenarios. This approach was adopted and publicized by Shell, at a time when their industry was also subject to enormous change and uncertainty. Shell planners asked managers to say how they would manage the business in certain conditions, giving them a variety of scenarios reflecting possible combinations of factors. At a time when the price of crude oil was over

$30 a barrel, one scenario was a market price of $15. Managers at first refused to react to this, as they thought it impossible and ridiculous. The planners persevered, and the managers did work through the scenario. As a result, they were somewhat better prepared than they otherwise would have been when the price actually fell to $13 a barrel.

By analogy, manufacturers should be working through a scenario which goes something like:

- Seventy per cent of the market goes through two or three retailers.
- Retailers' net profit margins are 10 per cent on sales.
- Retailers' brands account for 50 per cent of the market.

In some sectors such a scenario is not far off, and it is quite feasible in others which currently show quite different characteristics.

Again, the problem is to get away from our fixed mind-set and to produce scenarios which are 'unthinkable' in terms of the present business. People from within the firm probably cannot do this very well on their own, and outside experts will have to be used in addition. These could include editors and journalists from trade publications, consultants and of course retailers themselves. Opinions from those with vested interests will need to be sifted, and some consensus sought; total agreement is not necessary, as the idea is to produce more than one scenario reflecting differing possible outcomes.

To do the job properly we need to return to our diagnosis, and to identify the forces which are driving change in the system. These will include as a minimum:

- Demographics
- Social trends (including fashions, style and taste)
- Economic factors
- Government policies (legal, planning, fiscal)
- Technological change
- Structure of the retail trade
- Competition in the retail sector, including new entrants
- Structure of the manufacturing industry
- Competition in the industry, including new entrants

Some of these (such as demographics) are easier to forecast than others (such as changes in taste). Even with only a few possible variations in each, the total number of possible combinations is obviously huge, and some simplification will be needed. Most people would be happy with a selection of worst-case, most likely, best-case for a small number of scenarios.

Given the complexity and uncertainty, it is not to be expected that any one outcome can be selected as what will definitely happen. Planning therefore must be flexible, and any organizational solution must also be capable of adapting to changing circumstances.

3 Specification of tasks and roles

The next step is to try to specify as precisely as possible all the things that need to be done in managing the relationship with retail customers in order to survive and generate profit. Many of these are fairly obvious, but others may not be, especially those arising from radically new situations. If two or three scenarios have emerged as candidates (even worst-case candidates), then they should be examined for their implications as to task and role demands they would make.

In a book such as this, only broad generalizations can be made. Every firm will have special circumstances, its own history and culture; each will have to work out its own set of tasks. None the less, there are broad areas common to all, so let us look at these to try to tease out in particular the tasks that were perhaps not necessary in the past, but will in the future be vitally important.

First, let us look at what tasks were traditionally performed by the marketing and sales departments.

Marketing as a function has the goal of understanding the consumer and on that base building and maintaining strong brands. (At least, that is in my view the only proper definition of marketing's unique contribution to the business.) In order to meet this goal, marketing people carry out a variety of tasks related to the management of the elements of the marketing mix. These will include:

- Commissioning and interpreting market research.
- Managing the development of advertising campaigns.
- Planning and managing promotions.
- Recommending prices.
- Advising on product formulation and design.
- Managing pack design.
- Overseeing product development and testing.
- Liaising with production.
- Liaising with the sales force.
- Competitor analysis and the development of competitive strategy.

- Overall planning to put all the elements together in a coherent plan which will meet corporate objectives.

Sales departments have had as their goal shifting volume to retailers. This is to put it crudely, but accurately in my view. To achieve this, they carry out tasks such as:

- Building and maintaining a relationship with major retail customers.
- Negotiating sales to all customers.
- Taking orders, negotiating delivery schedules.
- Calling on individual stores (when allowed).
- Making presentations to customers.
- Liaising with marketing on promotions, new brand launches etc.
- Managing trade pricing structures.
- Reporting back intelligence on customers and competitors.

There is a host of other tasks such as arranging conferences and exhibitions, producing sales material and manuals, and so on; these need to be detailed by each firm. There are also basic management tasks of recruitment, selection and training, motivating and controlling etc. The selection and training aspects are likely to become more important in future.

Although some of the tasks listed above relate to customers, others have appeared in recent years which can be grouped under the term trade marketing, as a current shorthand.

Trade marketing tries to meet the new demands from an increasingly powerful retail trade. The term is so imprecise, and practice so varied, that there is no consensus on what tasks should be included. Some of the more obvious are:

- Providing advice on, and interpretation of, models such as DPP and space management.
- Coordinating customer intelligence.
- Representing the customer point of view to sales and marketing.
- Collating market data for presentations to customers.

Some companies have given much greater responsibility to a trade marketing group, as we shall see when looking at the options available.

The new demands of an altered customer relationship which are not covered by these traditional models fall under three headings which we could alliteratively call coordination, culture and control.

Coordination between marketing, sales and production functions has always been necessary, but in practice has often fallen far short of the ideal. The way in which retailers now operate has made this coordination even more important, and has added more people and functions which need to talk to each other. As we saw earlier, most of the manufacturer's departments are involved in some way and at some time in the relationship with customers. Therefore, their activities need to be coordinated so that they work together to a common goal, rather than against each other. Coordination and communication take time and cost money, but these must be balanced against the needs of the new way of doing business. Individuals must recognize that it is part of their responsibility to liaise and communicate with colleagues; and specific people need to be given the role of coordinating certain sets of tasks. Good information systems, open to all who need to use them, are at the heart of many of the dramatically effective management approaches of Japanese companies, and such systems could make a major contribution to the coordination and communication problem.

Culture, and the difficulty of changing it, were discussed in Chapter 7. To operate effectively in the new climate the efforts of a wide variety of people need to be focused on working with customers. This will not happen on its own. Again, although it can be argued that every individual must make the effort, someone senior must have the role of driving the change in culture.

Control has two aspects. The first is to ensure that programmes are actually implemented (carrying out a survey of customers' opinions, for example, or redesigning the ordering system). This is relatively straight-forward. The more difficult and complex is to make sure that the overall point is not lost sight of – that the firm must meet its objectives, and in particular make a profit. In responding to newly identified needs and newly formulated demands of customers, it is easy to initiate projects which will help customers without necessarily improving our profit (and which indeed may undermine both present and future profitability). Someone must have the task of monitoring customer-related activities and relating them to profit targets.

At the end of this part of the exercise each firm should have a list of all the tasks which need to be carried out and the roles to be filled, set against what people are actually doing now. It would be surprising if there were not some mismatch, with some people doing things which are no longer necessary, some tasks which are extremely important not being carried out at all, and a lack of clear lines of responsibility and accountability in at least some areas. With that in mind, we can go on to look at what options are open to us to remedy the situation.

4 Examination of options

In any decision, one option is always to do nothing, and this should be considered. It may be that most of the tasks that need to be carried out are already being done, and that only minor adjustments are needed. For companies operating successfully, the maxim, 'If it ain't broke, don't fix it' may apply. On the other hand, another maxim is, 'If it's working now, it won't be in three years' time'. Virtually everyone will need to make some changes, now or in the near future.

For those with more of a gap between the present structure and the ideal, the possible options need to be considered in the context of the firm's particular situation. Given every possible combination of sub-options, the variations are almost endless. What we shall look at here are certain key decisions, and some broad outline solutions.

A separate Trade Marketing department, or not?

One obvious reaction to the perceived need is to set up a new group charged with all or some of the new tasks which have emerged. In practice this can vary from a small group whose job is mainly to collate information for the sales force to a major new department with a board director. The first is, in my opinion, almost always merely paying lip service to the idea of working with customers, and is an excuse for not doing anything more radical. If the analysis above is correct, the shortcomings of a typical fmcg manufacturer are not going to be cured by such a minor effort. The new group will have little power or influence, many of the gaps in coordination will persist, and very little will change.

At the other extreme some firms have appointed a senior person at board level, with a department with specific responsibilities and authority. Nabisco in the UK brought in a high-level Trading Director (with experience of both retailing and manufacturing) and a number of Trade Development Managers each responsible for a product group. In between, firms have set up one or more groups with some sub-set of the tasks and with varying amounts of authority. In order to make any impact at all on ways of operating that have been hallowed by time, it is essential within this approach to give some definite authority to the trade marketing group, even if it is only that they must be consulted on certain changes such as prices and discount structures. Ideally any person or group will earn their own authority, but given the resistance likely to be found to any innovation, particularly one such as this which appears to take away autonomy, some up-front power is probably necessary.

In some cases it is clear that the new department is designed to work itself out of a job. The need for a radical change of culture is recognized, and only a radical new structure will achieve this, it is argued. After some time (usually unspecified), people throughout the organization will have adopted customer thinking, there will be a real focus on customer needs in all the relevant departments, and the Trade Marketing department will no longer be necessary. This cycle has already been gone through at United Biscuits (perhaps it is no coincidence that the company is so highly regarded by retailers in the UK), and others see it as likely to happen. It may, of course, take a considerable time, and at present some manufacturers such as Heinz are going in the opposite direction and increasing the size and power of the trade marketing unit. Each company needs to reach the solution which is right for its own particular situation.

Whatever the titles, there will definitely be a need for individuals or groups to be charged with certain sets of tasks which are either not done now, or are carried out less than perfectly. These will be examined under the headings of models, information, logistics and transactions.

- **Models**: by this we mean DPP, space management and other computer-based aids which may appear. Whatever one's views as to the real benefits of such approaches, they are undoubtedly here for now. Someone or some group must be given the task of understanding them and applying them to your business and your customers'. As has been pointed out, this may be both defensive and offensive. The worst situation will be for NAMs to be constantly caught out in ignorance. On the positive side, there is mileage to be made out of helping customers to apply the models to your product fields. Exactly how the function is set up will depend on the firm's size and resources. Some have a sizeable group, with all the available models. Of these, some offer a confidential service to customers, quite separate from any sales relationship (and presumably with Chinese walls between this group and the NAMs). In other companies, one person, often a former sales person with an aptitude for and interest in the topic, is in charge. The group or individual must be made responsible for training as well as actually carrying out the modelling, since NAMs and others must get themselves up to speed quickly with at least a familiarity with the bones of the models and their application.
- **Information**: we have seen that we need information on customers, and on markets and consumers. The last two are presumably already collected by the marketing department, but it must be decided who should be responsible for assembling the data and retrieving them for

use with customers. At present some companies allocate the job to a new group, while others allow juniors in the brand group to spend much of their time on it by default. In other firms the task is one of those which tends to fall between the cracks, and not get done at all. Again, it seems clear that someone must be given specific responsibility for this vital job. The person must have an understanding of customers and a grasp of data interpretation and presentation. In smaller companies this may form only part of one person's job, while in large manufacturers the task may be split between several people, each responsible for one or a group of accounts.

● **Logistics and transactions** may be taken together as they concern all those operations involved in receiving and processing orders, scheduling deliveries, dealing with invoicing and payment, and coping with all the queries and complaints that result from them. As the whole system is now much more integrated, these hitherto peripheral operations are much more central to the whole relationship with customers, and they need to be coordinated. Some companies have set up a group, sometimes called Customer Service, to carry out these tasks. The objectives set are to make the customer's job of ordering and paying as easy as possible, and to meet a given service level (e.g. 99 per cent of orders delivered in the correct amounts at the agreed time, or 95 per cent of orders delivered within forty-eight hours). A vitally important point to remember is that customer service levels must be defined as the customer defines them.

In one highly regarded manufacturer, the NAMs could not present their customer service results to the retailers, as the company's measurements were on a different basis from the customer's; the retailer would laugh when told that the supplier was achieving 95 per cent of target, when their own measurement suggested that the true figure was nearer 50 per cent. What was worse, it was politically impossible to change the manufacturer's system, because any change would produce a once-off drop in apparent achievement, and the director concerned was not prepared to see that happen. It has to be clear what exactly is being measured: percentage of what the retailer wants, or percentage of orders actually placed, for example. It is easy to show a high percentage of orders satisfactorily filled if you have told customers that you cannot supply their total needs – but it hardly reflects perfect customer service.

All the individual tasks are probably carried out already; what is new is the coordination and the focus on serving the customer. As mentioned earlier, the direct linking of manufacturer and retailer computer systems is driving wider cooperation between the two in many cases.

Category management and business teams

It will be clear that just setting up a new department with specific tasks and authority will go only some of the way to meeting all the problems outlined. A broader solution is needed. Two candidates are examined here.

The phrase 'category management' has appeared recently, especially in companies of American parentage. In theory it could mean that a whole category or product group is managed as an entity, with all functions coordinated to serve the needs of customers and consumers. Nationally advertised brands and retailers' brands could be included, since both are demanded by customers and bought by at least some consumers. The company could manage its brand and private-label portfolio to maximize sales, or use of production capacity, or profit (or, with extreme difficulty, all three).

The reality at present seems somewhat different, and the category management structures operating are little more than the old product groups, that is a number of brands whose managers report to a Product Group Manager. In other words, it is just one level in the hierarchy, and does not tackle, let alone solve, the problems of the new relationship with customers.

A broader approach is that of business teams, which do try to face up to the new needs directly. Over and over again, the need for coordination between departments has been stressed. The business team does this by regular meetings including not only sales and marketing, but production, distribution, accounts – everyone who has some impact on customers and who has some input to decisions. It is striking how this approach chimes with some of the themes of the new ways of doing business discussed at the beginning of this chapter. The Ford Car Program Management concept was given as an example, with all departments answering to the central hub. In an fmcg manufacturer, this could be real category management, with a category manager leading a business team, with profit responsibility for a discrete chunk of the company's business. The manager could come from any function, and would be a business person first, and a sales, marketing or production person very much second.

Obviously such a concept would take careful working out in practice, although the process could start with business team meetings for coordination only. This would be as non-threatening as possible, but would hopefully show participants the benefits. In the right atmosphere, they would want to develop the idea further themselves. All the evidence supports the view that giving small groups autonomy and responsibility for their own output is motivating and involving. Old, narrow ways of thinking, 'them and us' attitudes, departmentalization and 'not invented here', all disappear; efficiency and productivity increase, as does quality.

There are of course difficulties, not least those of physical production plant and location. The experience of companies which have applied the concept suggests that most barriers are in the minds of managers.

Customer focus and consumer focus

The main thrust of this book is that it is vital for manufacturers to develop a focus on their retail customers, a focus which has been missing so far in most cases. Without detracting from this in any way, it is also important to remember that the company must focus on consumers. The consumer focus is comparatively recent for most European companies, and it would be ironic if just as it was becoming established, attention were to be diverted away towards customers just because of the day-to-day pressures produced by retailer power. Any organization design must recognize this twin target, therefore.

It has been argued above that in some companies the demands of retailers have led to marketing people spending too much of their time and effort in supporting trade negotiations at the expense of their main task of building the brand. It is certain that in many product fields there has been a siphoning off of funds from major theme advertising to below-the-line spending, and a great deal of junior brand managers' time is spent on promotions. It is my view that sustained spending on promotions is not in the long-term interest of the brand, unless the promotions are extremely carefully tailored to supporting and enhancing the brand's core values in the eyes of target consumers. In how many cases is that true? In many companies, the marketing people argue that they have maintained the margin devoted to marketing spending; but the reality is that the margin is calculated from an assumed manufacturer's selling price before deduction of 'discounts' to retailers. These 'discounts' are in fact so well established and permanent that they represent money that the manufacturer never sees, and in fact does not really exist. When one adds the increasing proportion of the total marketing budget that has been going to trade promotion (and therefore not into above-the-line brand support), the proposition that marketing budgets have been maintained becomes a dangerous self-delusion.

This argument leads to the proposition that marketing people should not be concerned with promotions at all. They should concentrate on building an impregnable brand proposition, using market research to help them understand consumers in depth and advertising to communicate and sustain the core values. Close liaison with production would ensure delivery of the right quality of product. All other matters should be left to a customer-focused group which would combine the functions of NAMs, sales force, promotions (mainly geared to the trade anyway), trade marketing support and logistics.

A key feature here is the authority given to the NAM. It has been mentioned that retailers frequently complain that the person talking to them does not have the authority to make decisions. When the negotiations may cover not just prices and margins, allowances and promotions, but details of production, packaging and delivery, then it is not surprising that the NAM does not have the authority in the current system. In the new approach, the team would debate and decide on policy on all relevant issues (because they have the knowledge between them), and the NAM would be authorized to make detailed decisions. Empowerment is a fashionable term, suggesting that the people at the front end (whether of a production process or a service delivery) need to be given the authority to do what seems right to them at the time to produce the best results. That concept is absolutely right for this new approach to serving retail customers. Control must be kept within the team, but the front-line troops must be empowered to act within the guidelines laid down.

This view has an undeniable logic and appeal. It would be resisted by marketing personnel, who would see it as an attack on their authority and as a limitation on their sphere of influence. This is true, and consistent with other pressures on the primacy of marketing as a function.

On the other hand, it would concentrate the mind wonderfully, and the task remaining is by no means trivial. It is, on the contrary, an enormous challenge which will stretch the capabilities of the ablest. To create and sustain a major brand is one of the most difficult tasks in business. It demands intellectual skills of the highest order, an analytical grasp of complex data, the ability to empathize with consumers, a high level of creativity, and inter-personal and managerial skills. Surely this makes for a demanding and rewarding career?

To refocus the marketing function in this way does not conflict with the business team approach in any way, and indeed may be helpful in splitting up the tasks into manageable pieces.

Some possible structures

Some examples of organization structures which try to meet the numerous challenges outlined are shown in Figures 8.4–8.9.

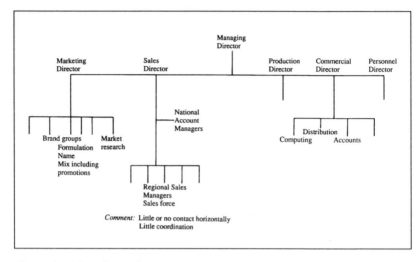

Figure 8.4 Traditional organization

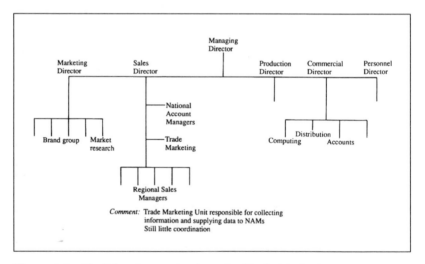

Figure 8.5 Traditional organization plus Trade Marketing Unit

5 Selection of best-fit solution

There is no one best solution which will fit any organization. Companies differ so much in size, complexity, history and culture that what will suit one would be quite wrong for another. Choosing what is best for your

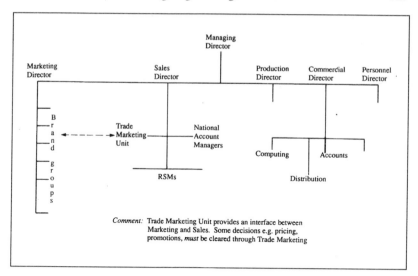

Figure 8.6 Trade Marketing Unit with increased power

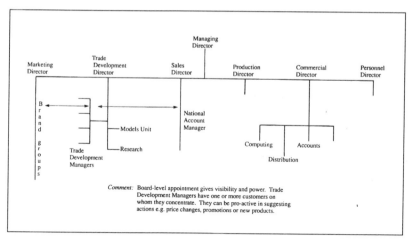

Figure 8.7 Trade Development Director

firm will demand sensitivity to its current position and to the demands of the future. Clearly smaller firms will have constraints that do not apply to larger ones, and one of the most dangerous temptations is to try to copy a format which has worked well in a huge multinational in a small national or regional company.

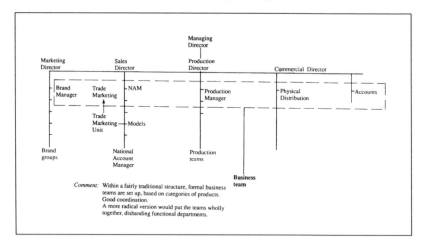

Figure 8.8   Business teams

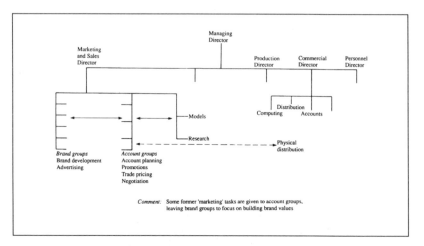

Figure 8.9   Separate account groups

One of the major choices depends on the gap between where you are now and where you want to get to; this will affect the radicalism and speed of implementation of your solution. There are times in the lives of most organizations when something very dramatic is needed, when everything must be turned upside down in order to produce any significant movement at all. This often coincides with the arrival of a new chief executive or new marketing director. At other times an organization needs slow and careful consolidation; revolutionary change would be disruptive and counterproductive. There are no sure guidelines in this difficult area. The decision calls for imagination as well as sensitivity on the part of the board.

Any solution chosen should be tested to check that it meets the criteria – does it give:

- Clear customer focus
- Clear consumer focus
- Coverage of all the tasks and roles enumerated
- Solutions to the problems identified in the diagnosis
- A realistic promise of delivering greater effectiveness
- A realistic promise of delivering greater profit?

The ideal is probably not attainable. Carrying out all the tasks one would like to do is unlikely to be the most profitable solution. On the other hand, trying to minimize costs is likely to lead to declining profits in the medium to long term. Given the overall pressure in most businesses to cut costs, and the usual freeze on head-count, it may be that a cost-effective way forward would be to identify some activities which are strictly short-term, and use outside consultants or short-contract employees for those. If a major change is needed, there is certain to be a bulge of workload and cost before benefits start to show through in improved volumes and margins.

6 Implementation

Project teams and task forces

Whatever the solution adopted, even doing nothing in terms of structure, new ways of thinking and better communication will be needed. One way of doing this is to set up cross-functional teams to study particular problems. The team members might or might not be relieved of their existing responsibilities, depending on the nature of the task. In any case, they would return to normal when the task was completed. This approach has been used successfully in a wide variety of situations, and seems particularly appropriate in this context.

The tasks would need to reflect the firm's priorities, and might include such topics as:

- Improving communications between sales and marketing.
- Implementing a new ordering system.

- Improving the relationship with (or profitability of) a particular customer.
- Identification of training needs of NAMs and sales people.
- Implications of information technology.
- DPP for specific products.

The advantages of task forces are that no major – and therefore unsettling – changes are introduced, that people can be involved in recommendations, that they learn experientially about the problems and priorities of other departments, that solutions are likely to be feasible within the company's culture and situation (unlike some outside consultants' reports, for example), and that the solutions are 'owned' by those who will have to implement them.

The task should be very carefully defined, specific action plans asked for, and a clear deadline set. The objectives and criteria for success should be challenging, but just possible (this is to avoid the danger of tunnel vision and unimaginative thinking). The phrase 'working party' should probably be avoided. Well managed, this approach could lead to successful change without too much upheaval.

The right staff

Customer service in its broadest sense must now have a high priority and profile. It follows that the people dealing with retailers must be of the highest calibre – as high as those dealing with brand development. Traditionally, in most fmcg companies marketing people are better qualified on entry than those in the sales function, and they tend to be accorded higher rewards and status throughout their careers. Typically, the average age of NAMs will be higher than that of marketing managers, and they will be of lower ability. This is no longer acceptable. The buying teams in retailers will be of high quality, and those dealing with them must be of equal competence and standing.

Very much more cross-fertilization must take place between sales and marketing, with young marketing managers spending a substantial time in the national account function – a minimum of two years, not just the usual six months as a rep during their preliminary training period; similarly, sales people should as a matter of course spend time in a brand group. The new role and status of the customer service function must be made clear by board attention, by promotion and reward systems and by any other cultural rituals that work in a given organization.

Training needs

Given that we have to start from where we are, changing an organization necessarily means retraining existing staff. A well-run company will already have a comprehensive appraisal system and training and development programme. Unfortunately, not all firms are well run in this respect. Recent reports have confirmed the UK's appalling record in management training: the average training received by British managers is less than a day a year. In the rapidly changing world of marketing to customers, this is totally inadequate.

Training needs should fall out of the match between the list of tasks and roles identified, and the set of people and skills available now. In the new organization, some people will have new tasks in their job description, some will have completely new roles. Apart from these specifics, there will be general needs. We can say with confidence that most companies which have got this far will have the following groups of training needs:

- General training across many or most departments to inculcate customer thinking and introduce the new way of working. For some sections intimately involved this may be quite intensive, and may be prolonged; for departments which are affected but are more peripheral half-day mass rallies may be enough. In all cases the training will need to be well planned, prepared for with newsletters or other publicity, and followed up with take-home material.
- Detailed training on new systems (planning, ordering etc.) for all those who will be operating them.
- Technical training on DPP, space management and other models as they appear for the sales force, and perhaps for support staff.
- Skills training for NAMs and sales people, particularly on presentation and negotiation.
- Interpersonal skills training for all those involved in business teams (group dynamics, listening skills, chairing and taking part in meetings).

Much of this may already be in place, but the comments of retailers suggest that many of the NAMs' skills need brushing up at least, and observation and experience suggest that most people could benefit from some training or up-dating in interpersonal skills.

The future: staff selection and development

The above is really about initial implementation, over perhaps the first year. Beyond that, the effort must not just stop. You need to be thinking and planning now for the future staffing and development of the relevant departments.

This can be done to some extent on the basis of the current reorganization, but also needs answers to questions about the future, such as, 'Will there be any field sales force?' In most cases, the sales role has changed irreversibly, and new sorts of people are needed. Some of the larger firms have recruited only graduates to the sales function for some years; will that be true for your company? There is no doubt that in general there will be fewer but more highly trained people, but exactly what sort of people will they be?

One feature of recent years has been the breaking down of barriers between sales and marketing in many companies. The new role of working with customers demands people who share some of the characteristics of traditional marketing as well as sales background. It is now not uncommon for marketing people to spend substantial parts of their career in a sales function (not just the old six months as a rep as part of their initial training programme). Equally, it could be valuable for a future NAM or sales director to spend time in a brand group as part of his or her development. All this needs planning, and has implications for recruitment and selection.

Summary

There are general influences on manufacturers' organizational structure which are prompting rethinking:

- The change in the balance of power between retailers and manufacturers.
- New methods of manufacturing.
- Internationalization.

Old systems are not always able to meet these new challenges, and new forms of organization are needed.

New methods of manufacturing include time-based competition (including just-in-time), flexible manufacturing systems, and total quality management. These approaches, apart from their direct benefits, make firms question established practices and structures.

International forces for change stem from the competitive drive for economies of scale.

All the influences put extra emphasis on the need for coordination and communication between functions.

Specific problems in dealing with customers reflect shortcomings in sales forces:

- Lack of expertise in computing.
- Lack of knowledge of production and distribution.
- Poor information-handling and presentation skills.
- Poor negotiation skills.
- Lack of authority to make decisions.

A step-by-step approach to redesigning the organization is recommended:

1 Diagnosis of the situation – where are we now?

- Company SWOT analysis and strategy development.
- Brand portfolio analysis.
- Diagnosis of retailer situation.
- Sales and marketing SWOT.

2 Prognosis – what is likely to happen?
3 Specification of tasks and roles – what needs to be done, and by whom?
4 Examination of options – what are the possible strategies and organizational structures open to us?
5 Selection of best-fit solution – which particular combination suits our situation, culture and resources?
6 Implementation – how do we travel from where we are now to where we want to get to?

Amongst the possible forms of organization discussed are business teams and category management, which offer many benefits relevant to the current situation. The business team should agree all the major policies, as it has the knowledge to do so. The NAM must be empowered to make tactical decisions within the policy guidelines.

Any solution chosen should be tested to check that it meets the criteria – does it give:

- Clear customer focus.
- Clear consumer focus.
- Coverage of all the tasks and roles enumerated.
- Solutions to the problems identified in the diagnosis.
- A realistic promise of delivering greater effectiveness.
- A realistic promise of delivering greater profit?

The use of project teams and task forces is recommended as a low-risk and effective way of implementing change.

The new approach adopted will have implications for training, and for future staff selection and development.

Further reading

Pascale, R. (1990), *Managing on the Edge*, New York: Viking

9
Building customers into planning and operation

In the fullness of time we might expect a company into which customer thinking has penetrated deeply not to have to worry about building customers into planning – it should happen automatically. For most manufacturers, that day appears still some way off. Even in firms which are trying to reorient themselves, there are still areas in which they could improve their service to customers or their effectiveness in marketing. In this chapter we will recapitulate the strategic issue, and then work through the elements of the marketing mix – the four Ps: product, price, promotion and place – as a reminder or checklist of points to bear in mind in working more closely with customers.

Strategic direction

It cannot be overemphasized that working with customers as a strategy cannot be seen in isolation from the company's overall strategic direction. The new power of retailers, together with the other pressures for change previously discussed, demand a response from the firm as a whole. Merely adding a new group, or reallocating a few sales people, and calling them 'Trade Marketing' is not the answer.

The firm must decide what sort of company it wants to be, and how it is going to compete. Do you want to be a strong leader, with big brands based on technological or marketing expertise; a niche player, avoiding direct confrontation with the big battalions by careful segmentation and positioning; a supplier of low-price brands, your own and retailers', relying on efficiencies in production for profit; or what? The decision on whether or not to make retailers' brands should be part of this overall strategic view.

Whichever strategy is adopted, it will be necessary to take a stance in relation to your customers. There is still a spectrum of possible stances:

- Strong independent
- Partner
- Responsive supplier

A prerequisite for the strong independent stance is the ownership – and the determination and ability to sustain – leading brands which retailers need to stock. This classic consumer marketing approach is still viable, although even here greater sensitivity to customers' as well as consumers' needs will be needed than was shown in the past by some manufacturers.

The partner approach is much talked about, and has had some clear successes in which manufacturer and retailer work together; as mentioned earlier, this has been helped and indeed driven by developments such as electronic data interchange (EDI). The concept is still looked on with suspicion by some managers in both manufacturers and retailers. Can it ever be a true partnership, when the two parties are to some extent at least competing for the available profit? It seems mainly a zero-sum game, in which one side's gain must necessarily be the other's loss. Or, if a particular national account manager (NAM) and buying team work well together and increase that supplier's sales through that retailer, this may appear a win-win situation: but has it merely taken some of the manufacturer's total sales from one retailer to another?

Experience in other sectors suggests that the traditional cynicism may be out of date. Part of the new approach to management referred to in the last chapter was the move to cooperative networks:

> Over the last few years, Xerox has slashed its suppliers from 5000 to about 350, and plans to cut the number further still. Each of the ones left is (or is becoming) Xerox's 'partner', each company aiming to make the other profitable. Paul Lawrence, of Harvard, calls this a value-added partnership (VAP). He cites as an example McKesson Corporation, an innovative, $6 billion San Francisco drug distributor: What makes McKesson so powerful – and what makes it a VAP – is the understanding that each player in the

value-added chain has a stake in the others' success. McKesson managers see
the entire VAP – not just one part of it – as one competitive unit. It was this
awareness that allowed them to look for opportunities beyond their own
corporate boundaries.

(Tom Peters, *The Economist*, 4 March 1989):

In other words, the old adversarial approach may appear to give short-
term gains to the buyer, but in the longer run both parties will be better
off working together; it will become a positive-sum game in which both
can win. 'Tell this to the retailers!', I hear the manufacturers cry, and
certainly they will have to change too. Some developments in just-in-time
deliveries and linking computers are forcing the parties to act together,
and as we have seen, wider cooperation is possible. To adopt a partnership
approach is compatible with having strong brands, of course, or with a
mixed branded/own-label strategy.

In one case, the NAM in a leading fmcg company and the head of the
relevant buying group in a major multiple have struck up a very close
working partnership. They are of a similar age (around thirty) and
background (graduates with significant marketing experience) and they talk
the same language. They have complete confidence in each other, and share
information which would in other relationships be regarded as very
sensitive. Working together, they have increased sales and profits of the
product group through those outlets. Both managements are happy with the
results, and with the nature of the relationship. It is possible for former
adversaries to act as partners, and for both to gain.

The third stance, that of the responsive supplier, could sound rather
weak-kneed, but the term is not intended to be pejorative. If the
manufacturer's SWOT (strengths, weaknesses, opportunities, threats)
analysis leads to the conclusion that a strong independent stance is not
sustainable, and indeed that few if any of the existing brands will survive,
then becoming a supplier responding to the powerful retailer is a perfectly
respectable strategy.

This leads on to a further question which adopters of either the partner
or responsive supplier stance will have to ask: should we aim to become
the preferred supplier of one particular retailer? There are clear dangers to
such an approach if it would make all the other retailers take retaliatory
action, but great potential benefits too. Whether it is worth considering
will depend on the structure of the market concerned. If there is one
dominant retailer with 50 to 80 per cent of a product field (and this is true

of some sectors), then it would be of enormous potential benefit to become the preferred supplier, always provided that the business was profitable. For the manufacturer, the ability to deliver quality and to maintain a high level of customer service would appear to be the crucial factors. It is difficult to identify situations in which a preferred supplier relationship exists, as both parties may wish to keep it confidential, though it is clear that the leading manufacturers in several sectors are working towards that position.

From the retailer's point of view, it is impossible to treat hundreds of suppliers as partners; the working relationship must be close and intense to have any impact, and that is time-consuming. It is therefore in a retailer's interest to choose a small number of manufacturers as partners and preferred suppliers. Such partners will be closer to their customer, will share with them new developments from both sides, and are likely to receive preferential treatment in space allocation. There may be a cost to the manufacturer, of course; but it is more likely to be a cost of flexibility and the giving of trust than one of money. Indeed, a preferred supplier ought to be earning more from the partner retailer than a competitor working in the old, adversarial way. Would you rather be a preferred supplier, or one of the rest? The answer seems obvious, but to get to the position of preferred supplier to a tough, professional retailer takes commitment from the top, and sweeping changes in attitudes, policies, and staffing.

Whatever decisions are taken as to the right stance for your company – and it is worth stressing again that there is no right or wrong answer in general – any manufacturer ought to adopt one key stance towards the retailers:

> We are the category experts. However much you know about your sales through your scanning systems, you know only about your own position, while we know about the market as a whole. Moreover, you stock so many products that you cannot possibly study and understand every one of them in detail. We operate only in one (or two, three. . .) product field(s), so we really know everything there is to know about it. Rely on us for expert advice about each category.

Let us assume then that the company has worked through its overall strategy. It has clear goals in terms of product/market scope, market position and branding. It has adopted a particular stance towards retailers which is compatible with these goals, and which will help attain them. Marketing objectives have been agreed for brand shares, volume and value of sales, range extensions, old and new product development. All these have been checked for coherence amongst themselves and fit with the company, competitors and the market. The task of detailed strategy and planning is to enable the objectives to be reached.

Strategy has perhaps become an overworked word in recent years. I use it to mean a set of guidelines for decisions. Thus a strategy to become a world low-cost manufacturer helps with decisions about proliferating specialities; a strategy of premium-quality branding helps with decisions about pricing. More specifically for this context, a strategy involving strong brands would – in my view – inform decisions about spending on advertising and promotion. The point is that decisions about the level and allocation of such spending should flow from consciously formed strategic views, and should not be mid-year reactions to a particular pressure situation.

Let us now look at each of the four Ps in turn.

Product

The usefulness of the old acronym of the four Ps is unfortunate in that we continue to use the wrong word not only for distribution, but also for brand. The distinction between product and brand is crucial, and cannot be emphasized too often. In terms of the whole company's thinking, it would be helpful to replace the word product by brand in every circumstance, in the same way that replacing the phrase 'the trade' by 'customers' signals an overall reorientation. This is true whether the brand is the manufacturer's or a retailer's.

Classically, a brand is developed and sustained by a fierce commitment to the closest match between consumers' changing wants and the multiple aspects of the brand under the manufacturer's control – delivery of functional benefits, psychological benefits, packaging, name, communications, availability, price and so on. This will not change.

What is new is that alongside this consumer focus will be the planned consideration of customers' needs too. This consideration will apply at a long-term strategic level – what sort of brands and ranges to make – as well as at the very short term, and at all levels in between. Often, the development of the best brand for consumers will also be best for retailers too. Unfortunately, there will also be occasions when the interests of consumers, manufacturers and and retailers conflict, and some trade-off will be needed.

A good example of conflict is range extension. Often an extension to a successful brand is the logical step for a manufacturer to take, and it can offer real benefits to consumers. To retailers, however, it can be a real problem as they have very limited space. The right way to deal with this problem was shown by Procter and Gamble in their launch of boy and girl Pampers disposable nappies (diapers). These are not just pink and blue, but have the absorbent material differently placed to match differences in anatomy (small, but important). The extension offers consumer benefits, and a clear advantage to the manufacturer in terms of sales, brand franchise and impact at point of sale. This last points up the problem for the retailer: the category is static in total sales in the USA (though not yet in the UK and other countries), so the extra space needed to display the new versions (by definition larger than before, if not necessarily twice as large), has to come from some other brand.

Procter and Gamble approached this in both the USA and the UK by carefully analysing the impact on retailers' layout, sales and profits before selling in. Their presentation to customers could therefore anticipate probable objections, and provide answers. In fact, they went further and designed the packaging so that the packs could be displayed in different ways to optimize shelf space while ensuring that the logo could always be read.

This example suggests that the consideration of retailers' needs should start very early, and run right through the decisions that make up overall product and brand policy. Let us look at them in turn.

New brand development

This is understandably a very sensitive area. Manufacturers complain that retailers demand increasingly long lead times before they will give new brands shelf space, and then allow decreasingly short trial time in which the new brand has to prove itself. Retailers reply that manufacturers do not consult them, and therefore make elementary errors leading to an unacceptably high rate of failure. As has been pointed out before, cooperation is possible, and is successfully practised by some manufacturers and their customers; others on both sides are sceptical.

The increasing availability of scanning data will strengthen retailers' hands in terms of ability to measure sales performance quickly and accurately. Widespread provision of integrated data systems (linking scanning data with consumer debit cards and possibly media exposure) will mean that some form of cooperation becomes inevitable. The questions will still remain, 'To what extent should retailers' needs be built into the new brand development process, and how early should they be consulted?'

The answers given will depend on the stance vis-à-vis retailers taken up, and on the particular circumstances. A strong independent stance will lead to relatively late and little consultation, and the evidence is that this is acceptable to retailers. It emphatically does not mean that no thought is given to retailers' needs, as the Procter and Gamble example above shows. It simply does not make sense any more not to build consideration of customers into the new brand development process from the very beginning. Expensive mistakes and mis-calculations can be prevented early on; from a more positive angle, new opportunities can be identified which might otherwise be missed.

Early on, then, basic questions need to be asked. This may be as early as the concept testing stage, and certainly by the stage of preliminary business analysis. Up to 70 per cent of all development money is spent on projects which do not end up as viable new brands, so it is vital to build in this extra check before too much time and money are committed.

The sort of questions are:

- How would this brand fit in with our major customers' overall strategies? Would it help their strategic development, fill a gap, duplicate existing provision?
- What would be the effect on their sales and profitability (taking direct product profitability (DPP) and space management into account)?
- What shelf space would it need? Where in the store? How would this affect the rest of their business?
- Would it make any special demands on them, in terms of buying, storage, display, promotion or support? If so, how would we propose to help?
- What packaging would be most attractive to our customers as well as to consumers? Can we make the configuration of outers, traded units and individual packs as efficient as possible right through the distribution chain?
- What are our customers' views on sizes, varieties etc?
- Where does our proposed pricing fit into our customers' existing and desired structure?

Many of these questions are of course much easier to ask than to answer. Many will throw up possible conflicts with consumer needs, or with our own objectives. It is nevertheless vital to pose them, and to do so before important decisions are set in concrete. This is true whatever the manufacturer's strategic position. Many manufacturers have NPD policies which build in checklists at various stages; a version of the questions listed above should be added to the checks that a new brand has to pass through.

The issue of timing is more flexible. In some circumstances, considerations of secrecy will demand that retailers should not be informed until the last moment. Manufacturers can be very sensitive indeed about confidentiality, and are cynical about the ability of outside agencies and customers to keep other people's secrets. Retailers of course find this slightly insulting, if understandable. The answer is greater trust, but this takes time to build up, and anyway is not a complete solution. When manufacturer A approaches a customer and tells him of an impending new brand launch, no one would expect the customer to reply, 'Oh, B is just about to launch an identical product.' As in many other parts of the relationship, there will always be grey areas, and zones where secrecy and arm's-length dealing prevail. In general, the better the overall relationship, the more open we should expect discussions of new brand development to be, and this ought to be seen as desirable.

Range and portfolio

Apart from new brand development, manufacturers have to take many other decisions about their brands. These include:

- Corporate product portfolio.
- Width, depth and consistency of product lines.
- Existing brand development and modification.
- Positioning.
- Product deletion.

All these may have some impact on customers and the relationship with them. As a corollary, changes and developments in customers may have an impact on our brands, and we need to take that into account.

The point has been made before, and so perhaps does not need labouring; but the retailer dimension must be taken into account in all these decisions, and at present in many companies it simply is not. Obviously, information is basic to such decisions, in this case information on brand and range profitability by customer and customer group. Both long- and short-term questions should be asked, for example:

- Given the changes in retailing which we foresee over the next five years, what will our sales and profits look like if we carry on as we are? What threats do likely developments pose to our brands? What opportunities may arise and how might we take advantage of them? Examples of changes include increased concentration, increased pressure on space, new forms of retailing, new outlets, electronic funds transfer at point of sale (EFTPOS) and tele-shopping.

- For each customer, how is their positioning changing, and how does that match with the way our brands are moving in the market? Will planned developments in our target segments and positioning be helped or hindered by changes in retailers?

- In the medium term, what are shoppers' core values, what are they looking for in this category and how is this changing? Does it vary between different retail chains: are Tesco shoppers looking for something different from Safeway shoppers, or BhS shoppers from Littlewoods? How might we exploit such differences and adapt our brand offerings to changing shopper needs? It is here in detailed knowledge of consumers that manufacturers can demonstrate their category expertise and be proactive towards their customers: 'Look, this is what is happening to consumers – your customers – and this is how we can help you to take advantage of it.' As mentioned earlier, manufacturers also need to understand better – perhaps in partnership with the retailer – the intriguing differences between the way shoppers appear to use the different multiples.

- Short-term questions are likely to be very specific. Why are we losing stocking units (SKUs) in this category in Sainsbury's? If medium-sized Spar stores will only take 20 SKUs of soup when we have 70 on our own in wholesalers, which varieties and sizes should we offer? Here the overlap with the 'place' of the four Ps is clear, and the account planning function needs to be working well however the firm is organized.

Price

Traditionally, price has been one of the main negotiating points between manufacturers and retailers, and this will not change. Despite the apparent increased importance of other aspects of the total relationship, price and gross margin remain dominant issues for most buyers. Often it is in the manufacturer's interest to divert attention to the other aspects, particularly brand quality and uniqueness; successful branding creates a temporary local monopoly which allows the manufacturer more freedom in resisting retailer pressure on price and margin. However, most of the time for most brands, the buyer is trying to squeeze extra concessions on price, whether directly or indirectly.

This causes two sorts of problems for manufacturers: the obvious one of downward pressure on profits, and the indirect one of the difficulty of controlling a carefully designed marketing mix. Price is seen by marketing people as an integral part of a complex, interacting whole which forms the brand offering to a target segment of consumers. It is an indicator of value, and positions the brand against its competitors. In this situation, it is irritating to say the least that the manufacturer can no longer control the final consumer price in the way that used to be possible. Retailers use prices as an important competitive weapon, and can put specific brand prices up and down in ways and at times that manufacturers cannot control.

> A dramatic example of this occurred in 1992 in the UK when discount drugstore chains started to offer premium *haute couture* perfumes at very significantly reduced prices. The manufacturers were furious, as the very high prices of their brands is an important part of their positioning. They tried to stop supplies to the offending retailers, but were unsuccessful (grey markets exist in most distribution channels). Other retailers had to choose whether to follow, or resist; most, understandably given the high margins they receive, resisted. A similar battle started in 1993 in the sun-care sector. Retailers argue that the very high prices charged in these product fields are not justified, and that if they wish to reduce their margins in their competitive struggle, they will benefit consumers as well as themselves. The manufacturers naturally do not see it that way. It is not yet clear what the final result will be. It is at least possible that price-cutting in markets such as premium perfumes will destroy or seriously harm the brands; high price and exclusivity are essential elements in the mystique. The real lesson for manufacturers is that they cannot control the retail price, and that must be factored into their strategies.

The position is more sensitive for KVIs, or known value items. These are brands that are staples and for which the consumers have a good idea of the prevailing price; Heinz Baked Beans are a good example. Each major retailer has to keep to the expected price or risk losing custom. The retailers therefore expect manufacturers to control the price to all their customers so that a rival cannot gain an advantage by offering a lower price on a key item.

This is of course the stuff of negotiation, and probably takes up a substantial amount of account managers' time. There is no simple answer which will make the problem go away.

The key question for manufacturers is how to gain, or regain, or maintain control. The ideal position is to have strong brands which consumers demand, and to set prices and discount structures which give retailers and the manufacturer fair profits. This of course begs the central question of what is a fair apportionment of the total profit available between the two parties. It comes back to the issue of power, and the party with the greater power in a particular situation will expect to earn the greater reward. The only way manufacturers can maintain power against increasing retailer concentration is, as has been said so often, to build unique brands and to support them. That apart, what can be done? These are some of the ways successful firms approach the problem. Some may appear banal or superficial, and some counsels of perfection; all are worth considering.

Reduce manufacturing costs

Most manufacturers at least pay lip service to this idea; some pursue it fanatically as a major plank in their strategy. For everyone, whether niche player or mass marketer, focused, differentiated or straight low-cost producer, the aim of keeping manufacturing costs to a minimum within their overall marketing strategy must be sensible. Production efficiencies provide a cushion which gives pricing much more flexibility. This applies right through the procurement–manufacturing cycle.

Reduce distribution costs

It follows that the same approach applies to the downstream parts of the system, that is storage and physical distribution. The greatest efficiencies can be achieved only through cooperation with customers who themselves operate a just-in-time system. Equally, of course, the demands of customers can in themselves produce higher costs unless the system is well understood and controlled. One major retailer demanded that their suppliers keep two weeks' stock at all times: the real costs of this would have been enormous for the manufacturers, and those who understood that refused to comply. Again, information becomes enormously important, and a good understanding of the principles of DPP is essential.

Develop good information systems

Efficiencies cannot be measured without information, and decisions taken either at leisure or in the heat of negotiation must be based on accurate data. As mentioned earlier, accounting data are not always well understood by marketing people, who must make special efforts to ensure that they get the data they really need, and that they grasp the reliability and implications of the data they use.

Train and inform NAMs

A frequent complaint from retailers about NAMs is that they are ill-informed and unable to take responsibility for decisions. Negotiations about price are now likely to range over total costs, not just item/case price and gross margin. The negotiator must be well informed about his or her own brand cost structure (through all its stages), but also about the probable costs of the retailer and of competitors. They must also be trained and able to take decisions which can be made to stick.

Publish open price lists

Some, mainly large, manufacturers publish price lists showing a standardized discount structure, and make it clear that they will not deviate from these terms. Others publish a price list but are known to give various deals, whether straight price reductions or disguised subsidies. It is generally accepted that the open price list has many advantages, and makes negotiation much simpler. Some manufacturers feel that for them such a practice is desirable but in practice impossible, given the pressure put on them by their large customers; again, it comes back to relative power. It must be seen as the desired objective, to be worked towards even if not immediately attainable. Whatever the current position, the budget available for special deals should be fixed for each brand, and the authority for using it clearly defined. This also applies to promotional allowances (see below).

Work with the retailer on a category

Using your position as the category expert, work with a particular customer on getting the best return for him or her from a particular category. Using the retailer's data and your knowledge of the market, and applying space management models, examine the stocking and layout policy in depth. This may lead to price adjustments as well as shelf allocation decisions, and may give opportunities to look at the margins across a number of brands. This may of course lead to a short-term lowering of price, but overall should improve returns for both parties.

> One manufacturer carried out a detailed space management study for a retailer on a particular category in two stores. The results showed that the field was over-stocked, with wrong space allocation, despite the fact that the retailer had thought it was efficiently managed. By manipulating cube space allocation and reducing linear, some brands which might have lost distribution were kept. The only way actually to increase the category's profitability was to give increased margin on the manufacturer's major brand – but the total effect was greater profit for both.

Keep in touch with consumers' perceptions

Price is seen as an indicator of value, but perceptions change both absolutely and relatively. The manufacturer must be in tune with the target group's feelings about price, and in particular be confident about what premium they are prepared to pay for the extra benefits offered by the brand. Recent years have seen many markets develop a bi-modal or 'schizophrenic' pattern, with increasing interest among consumers in high-priced, premium-quality brands and in low-priced economy brands, with the middle of the market suffering. In the early 1990s, some commentators have detected a swing against brands, particularly premium brands (see the discussion in Chapter 2). There has been a considerable amount of journalistic comment, especially in the USA, to the effect that after the excesses of the 80s consumers are turning away from over-hyped brand names, and looking for 'real' value for money. The Marlboro example shows clearly that manufacturers cannot be too greedy, and that they must always offer value; that should be axiomatic. The answer of Procter and Gamble has been to adopt a new 'everyday low price' strategy, offering a lower level of price across the range of their brands – but accompanied by a dramatic reduction in the amount of promotional allowances granted. This is a development of the open price list approach, and offers a clear simplification of the negotiating situation; whether other, smaller manufacturers could impose it is another matter.

Whether the early 90s position represents a real turning point, or is merely a reflection of the years of recession suffered by both the USA and UK, remains to be seen. Such trends offer both problems and clear opportunities, and manufacturers must keep their fingers on the pulse.

Promotion

The issue of promotional funds and who should control them has been touched on many times. It is taken as read here that the roles taken in promotion reflect brand strength and relative power. A strong brand will be supported by a high advertising budget, and the manufacturer will be relatively dominant in the relationship. With a weaker brand, the retailer will be more dominant, a higher proportion of the total budget will be devoted to below-the-line promotion, and advertising will fall. In some markets this process has been seen as a vicious spiral, with less and less advertising support for brands leading to a progressively weaker position, leading to less advertising support. . .and so on. Such a process leads to retailer dominance, high shares for retailers' brands, and in the worst cases to an overall decline in the total market size.

The arguments in this area are often emotional and hard information was difficult to find. In recent years, with new techniques of data gathering, some evidence has started to appear. This evidence, already referred to in Chapter 2, shows that:

● advertising's effects last for two or three years beyond the original campaign;
● only a minority of sales promotions are profitable when all costs and forward buying are taken into account;
● heavy trade promotion works against the effect of heavy advertising;
● there is, on the other hand, positive synergy between consumer promotion and heavy advertising.

As discussed in Chapter 2, the logic suggests that too much below-the-line promotion is dangerous for a brand. Unless it is very carefully targeted and coherent with the central brand proposition, continued promotions are saying to the consumer:

> The central benefits of this brand are not really sufficiently attractive to make you want to buy it all the time, so here are a few irrelevant inducements.

This is not to deny the usefulness and power of correctly designed promotions, but to cast doubt on the sloppy and thoughtless use of the tool, particularly when retailer pressure makes it the easy option in a difficult trading situation. To count discounts and allowances, along with trade and consumer promotion, as part of the total marketing budget is self-deluding. It is absolutely essential to retain a clear view of what money is going to support the brand, and what is going into the retailers' pocket.

To repeat the textbook but still correct assertion, the various elements of the marketing mix must be targeted to achieve the company's objectives. The differing roles of theme advertising, consumer promotion, and trade promotion must be understood, and they must be used in a way which is coherent and which fits the market and competitive situation.

Most strong brands will continue to need consistent support from theme advertising which encourages trial, and reinforces the beliefs of existing users. Despite the jeremiads of some prophets who claim that new technology and changing social patterns will make it impossible to apply classic mass market branding in a few years' time, no alternative has yet been suggested. Advertising methods may have to be adapted, but it will remain the main tool for building and maintaining strong brands outside the product itself.

There is of course a role for consumer promotions in the marketing of even the strongest brand, a role which is mainly tactical and which needs to be carefully planned. The retailers must be involved, since most promotions necessarily require their cooperation, but it should be the manufacturer who decides on the purpose of and budget for the schemes.

Trade promotions *a fortiori* need negotiation with customers, but again must be designed by the manufacturers and have specific targets. The size and disposition of the budget must be fixed, and clear responsibility allocated for decisions on spending. It is within this sometimes murky area that difficulties arise, since retailers' demands for a greater share of the profit available are often disguised as arguments for efficiency: 'We could do this (marketing) job for you more efficiently. . . .' Strong firms resist such demands; they may negotiate on what is the right package for a particular customer, but not on the amount. As suggested above, it is almost certainly in the manufacturer's interest to reduce trade promotion if that stance can be sustained in the face of retailer pressure.

These questions on promotion refer one back to the issue of how the marketing and selling tasks are organized, and who makes which decisions. It should be clear that all the marketing mix decisions are inter-related, and cannot be considered in isolation. That said, there is a strong case for saying that above-the-line advertising, as the main support for building the brand, must be the preserve of the brand group, while promotions should be the responsibility of an account planning group who focus on customers, as argued in Chapter 8.

Place

This whole book is about the interface between manufacturers and retailers, so anything said here is by way of summary. The major arguments are repeated below:

● Customer thinking must penetrate deep into all parts of the company.
● Staff in all departments must see the system as a whole and understand how the elements of the system inter-relate – procurement, manufacturing, marketing, selling, physical distribution, ordering, invoicing – all are part of one system.
● Decisions in all parts of the system, and especially in those closest to the market, must be made with customers' needs in mind.
● The right information must be available to the relevant people for such decisions to be made on a sound basis.
● Organization structure and planning systems must ensure that the firm takes a proactive stance towards customers so that the firm retains control of its own destiny.

Such statements can appear bland or high-flown. Concrete examples of what they mean in practice are scattered through the book – use of DPP, shrink-wrapping trays to save time in store, designing the assortment of varieties in a traded unit to match a customer's sales pattern, changing recruitment and training programmes for NAMs – the possibilities are endless. The challenge for the individual manufacturer is to work through the organization checking that all the possibilities are looked at, that threats are minimized and opportunities grasped.

Putting it together – the annual account review

The annual brand plan and review is standard practice in many firms, with the brand group presenting and defending its plan before senior management. Some manufacturers have adapted this, and give an annual review to their larger customers.

This seems an excellent idea, but unfortunately the reality is often less impressive. Retailers complain that presentations are overlong, excessively manufacturer-oriented, a rehash of old data, and a waste of their time. The addition of DPP and space management models can add some temporary interest, but again the glamour is too often spurious.

Let us assume that an internal review of each major account and customer group is essential, and will look at much the same things as the brand review – current situation, last year's actual against plan, reasons for variances, competitive situation, objectives for next year, plan and budget for sales volume and value, profit, promotions, special initiatives. Is it worth the time and trouble of making a special presentation to the customer? The answer must be that if you can't find anything useful to say, don't bother.

The question should therefore be recast: 'What would our customers like to know which we could tell them?' As has been said, the manufacturer's advantage ought to be in detailed knowledge of consumers and the market as a whole. Interesting and new research on trends in consumers' thinking, on shoppers' views of the different chains in this market, on their feelings about shopping in general, data on social changes, possibly on developments in other markets or other countries, might all be of interest. These could then be linked to a review of the particular relationship, with some judicious comparisons, leading to proposals for the coming year. The proposals should address the retailer's concerns, not just the manufacturer's, and might include joint projects in areas of mutual interest. The challenge in Chapter 3 is particularly relevant here: see yourself as your customer sees you. What does your business mean to them? Where is the profit coming from? How can you improve it? What specific efforts can you make to meet this customer's particular needs?

If there is little new to be said – and that may legitimately be the case in some years – then no formal presentation need be made. On the other hand, it is to be hoped that the manufacturer will have something important to say to customers fairly frequently, or it may rightly be concluded that the lead role has passed to retailers, leaving the manufacturer as a reactive supplier. The fault then is his or her own.

Summary

In time, customer thinking will become automatic, but for the present most manufacturers would benefit from checking through all the ways in which they could work more closely with retailers.

The overall strategic direction of the firm will determine much else. In relation to retailers, is it a:

- Strong independent
- Partner
- Responsive supplier?

Whatever stance adopted, the manufacturer should always be the category expert.

It is helpful as a summary to use the four Ps of marketing (product, price, promotion, place), although the acronym's neatness hides some distortions.

In place of product, we should think of brand, since it is in the strength of brands that many manufacturers' future lies. Even for brands, a new customer focus must be added to the consumer focus on which its success depends. There are sometimes conflicts between the two, as for example in the case of range extensions. Careful preparation of a case for retailers is even more important when a range extension appears to benefit the manufacturer but to offer little or nothing to retailers.

In new brand development, more cooperation with retailers is desirable. Early on, questions should be asked about a proposed new brand:

- How would this brand fit in with our major customers' overall strategies? Would it help their strategic development, fill a gap, duplicate existing provision?
- What would be the effect on their sales and profitability (taking DPP and space management into account)?
- What shelf space would it need? Where in the store? How would this affect the rest of their business?
- Would it make any special demands on them, in terms of buying, storage, display, promotion or support? If so, how would we propose to help?
- What packaging would be most attractive to our customers as well as to consumers?
- What are our customers' views on sizes, varieties etc.?
- Where does our proposed pricing fit into our customers' existing and desired structure?

Range and portfolio decisions also need to take customers into account.

Price will remain a major negotiating point, and there are no easy answers to continuing retailer pressure (apart from strong brands). Manufacturers should check through actions that could help:

- Reduce manufacturing cost.
- Reduce distribution cost.
- Develop good information systems.
- Train and inform NAMs.
- Publish open price lists.
- Work with the retailer on a category.
- Keep in touch with consumer perceptions.

With promotion, the issue will remain 'Who controls the spending?' Strong brands will need consistent support above the line; weaker brands will be forced to provide funds for the retailer to spend.

Retailers must be involved in planning consumer promotions, since most promotions necessarily require their cooperation, but it should be the manufacturer who decides on the purpose of and budget for the schemes.

Trade promotions *a fortiori* need negotiation with customers, but again must be designed by the manufacturers and have specific targets.

Annual account reviews should address the customer's concerns, not just the manufacturer's, and should show how that customer's specific needs will be addressed.

10
Internationalization

1992 and all that

In the late 1980s the year 1992 achieved a talismanic status in the minds of many in Europe – and indeed in Japan, America and elsewhere. 1992, like other symbolic years – 1066, or 1789 – stood for something. Like them, it appeared at first sight to represent something fairly simple and clear-cut; like them, it was in fact a symbol of a more complex reality.

To focus on one year and the specific changes it summarized was perhaps useful as a communication device to concentrate people's minds on a trend which had been developing momentum over a number of years – the internationalization of business. Now that the 1st January 1993 has passed and the Single Market has come into force (in theory if not yet wholly in practice), we can concentrate on the realities of the European – and indeed the world – market. Theodore Levitt, with his matchless flair for crystallizing and publicizing an issue, had trumpeted the coming globalization of markets. The arguments have raged back and forth about how useful such grand generalizations were to business managers, with evidence from all sides that markets are becoming more similar and that they remain different.

What this chapter will try to do is to look at the trend towards internationalization in consumers and in retailers, and at the implications of EC moves towards a true common market, in order to draw some conclusions as to how manufacturers may respond.

Changes in consumers

The Levitt view of globalization is posited on a convergence of cultures: people are becoming more and more the same all over the world (or at least in the industrial world). The success of brands such as Coca-Cola is evidence of this. On the other hand, it is clear that large differences still remain, even within a relatively compact and homogeneous area such as Europe. What firm evidence is there for either point of view?

Naturally, marketing people, especially in advertising agencies, have tried hard to identify international types of consumer. A typical attempt was that developed from French lifestyle surveys by CCA International.

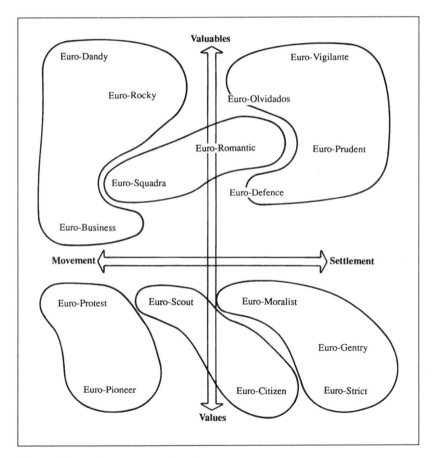

Figure 10.1 European sociostyles

This claimed to identify 16 'sociostyles' amongst Europeans, plotted on two axes – Movement to Settlement one way, and Values to Valuables the other. Thus the Euro-Gentry group are at the Settlement end of the scale and towards the Values end: they are conservatives who dislike pickets and demonstrations, and prefer martial music to rock'n'roll or jazz. At the opposite corner of the map are Euro-Rocky types, who are xenophobic, have little sense of social responsibility and are happy to live in a social jungle. The complete list is shown in Figure 10.1.

The problem with this is relating its results to consumer behaviour in a particular market. Knowing that Spain has large numbers of Euro-Pioneers and Euro-Citizens, who initiate change and development, while Britain has large numbers of Euro-Stricts, -Prudents, -Gentry and -Rockies, who resist change, is fascinating. What action implications it has for marketing is less clear. Like all such lifestyle studies, experience suggests that the technique will work for some markets, but will offer little illumination in others. Many marketing people argue that this is necessarily so, and that it makes sense to analyse each market separately, and each country separately. Market-specific segmentation studies may offer the best compromise.

Most people with experience of international markets would agree that there is a discernible movement to greater homogeneity between people. Within Europe in particular, and especially among the young, common patterns are emerging which have implications for both manufacturers and retailers. This does not mean that standardized European brands and campaigns can be introduced without thought and research. For example, in most European countries people who eat pasta frequently are at the leading edge of social trends, but in Italy they would be backward. Some of the trends noted lead towards greater disaggregation, not homogeneity. Overall, greater internationalization is on the way, albeit at different speeds in different markets.

Certainly, patterns of spending seem to be converging, despite wide gaps between the richest countries and the poorest. The well-known tendency is for a lower proportion of the household budget to be spent on food as income rises, and the EC average is getting closer to those of Japan and the USA.

Language differences alone mean that a single European market is some way off. Although there is no longer a legal need within the EC to translate labels from one EC language into others, much marketing material will need to be, for obvious reasons. Procter and Gamble's Pampers have packs large enough to carry eight languages (and can therefore be manufactured in a single factory for Europe); smaller packages such as confectionery have clear limitations (Ogilvy and Mather

SHARE OF DISPOSABLE BUDGET ACROSS EC 1988 vs 1970

	EC %	USA %	Japan %
EC trend down			
Food	21	13	21
Clothing	8	6	6
Equipment	8	6	6
EC trend up			
Accommodation	17	20	19
Transport	15	15	10
Leisure	8	10	10
Health	7	15	11

(Source: Eurostat)

1992). The language issue also means that so-called European media such as satellite television will be of limited value (although those who watch international sports broadcasts will see the rationale behind Mars' adoption of Snickers as a single brand name: a hoarding at a football match televised throughout Europe can remind all viewers of the brand name without the need for translation).

One suggestion is that in the short to medium term, there will be three types of brand in Europe: Euro-Masses, Euro-Niches and Locals (Ogilvy and Mather 1992). The Euro-Mass brands will succeed in markets in which the majority of consumers have preferences (or can be converted to them) which are common. Such markets are petrol, toiletries and pharmaceuticals, basic food and drink, some household goods, non-fashion clothing and small appliances. Euro-Niche brands will appeal to a defined segment which will be found in all markets, though possibly varying in size from country to country; specialist foods (baby, health or diet, connoisseur or 'foodie' products), hobby products, fashion clothing and cosmetics, perhaps garden products, are examples of this type. Locals are self-explanatory, and strong local brands with an appeal deep in the local culture seem certain to survive. The trick for manufacturers will be to diagnose which markets are ready for which brands; timing will be sensitive, and crucial.

International retailing

The 'retailing revolution' is a worldwide phenomenon. The trend to self-service is seen everywhere and in most product fields. The number of stores has declined dramatically in most countries, certainly in food retailing and to some extent in other markets. In general, the average size of store is increasing, with hypermarkets, superstores, DIY 'sheds' becoming more and more common.

Top ten organizations	Turnover (%)	Key decision points
High concentration		
Australia	97	11
Finland	94	5
Switzerland	90	14
Sweden	89	9
Denmark	89	7
Canada	88	59
Austria	84	36
Germany*	81	108
New Zealand	80	23
Medium concentration		
Netherlands	79	25
Belgium	66	
UK	66	12
France	62	145
Ireland	51	6
Low concentration		
Mexico	41	10

Nine others including USA, Italy, Spain, Japan *excluding Aldi

Figure 10.2 Concentration of food buying, Source: Nielsen, *Annual Marketing Review*, 1988

In terms of this book's focus, concentration of power in the hands of retail multiples is also widespread. In food, three countries – France, Belgium and Brazil – had four-fifths of their turnover in the leading 10 per cent of stores by 1986, according to A. C. Nielsen. A further nine countries, including the UK, had around two-thirds.

If we look at concentration of buying power in terms of key decision points, it is clear that in food, the pattern is also widespread (Figure 10.2).Thus there is variation in the degree of concentration even within one market, and variation between different markets. There is also a slight countertrend towards specialist smaller outlets. Overall, though, it can be said with confidence that in the Western world, retailers are looking more and more alike, whatever country one is in. Does this mean that retailing is therefore becoming international?

It has been striking that on the whole, the answer is no. Very few truly international retail chains exist. Even the great Marks and Spencer, which for many years seemed unable to do wrong in terms of retailing skills, has found it notably hard to transfer those skills outside the UK. Eventually it has made money elsewhere, but it has taken many years of losses and mistakes. One apparent exception, Benetton, is *sui generis*, being a hybrid of manufacturer, retailer and franchisor. Other successes such as the privately-owned C & A or the Swedish IKEA are the exceptions. Only in fast-food operations has there been truly international retailing established as a norm. Given that most retailers have traditionally sourced on an international basis, this is paradoxical.

It is of course true that some of the major multiples have bought chains abroad. Usually these seem to be more for the purpose of learning the retailing skills thought to be displayed in the host country – such as the USA – rather than as an extension of the purchaser's own. It is also true that as the leading multiples found it increasingly difficult to find continuing growth in their home country, they were forced to look outside.

In the late 1980s this trend began to take off. Outright mergers and acquisitions remained rare, except for a continuing interest amongst European firms in buying American chains (the weakness of the dollar had a lot to do with this). Elsewhere, acquisition seemed expensive, or was made difficult by local legal protection. Where it did happen, as with Boots' purchase of the French beauty chain Sephora, there seemed to be considerable difficulties in getting the two sets of managers to work together: there are cultural gaps amongst managers as well as consumers. This may be a specifically British problem, since it should be said that French and German retailers have been much readier to expand in other European countries, though still relatively slowly.

Some cross-border expansions have been:

Group	From	To
Aldi	Germany	Austria, Belgium, Denmark, France, Holland, UK
Tengelmann	Germany	Austria, Holland, Hungary, UK, Italy
Auchan	France	Spain, Italy
Docks de France	France	Spain
Comptoirs Modernes	France	Spain
Cora	France	Belgium
Marks and Spencer	UK	France, Spain, Holland, Belgium

(Source: Europanel)

What has been seen is a dramatic growth in alliances, either the setting up of buying groups or formal cross-purchase of minority shareholdings. In the most prominent, the Argyll group of the UK set up the European Retail Alliance with Koninklijke Ahold of the Netherlands and Groupe Casino of France; the group now includes Dansk Supermaked, ICA (Sweden), Kesco (Finland), Rinascente (Italy), Mercadona (Spain) and Migros (Switzerland). They claim to have 11 per cent of the market in these countries, with sales of ECU 35 billion (Ogilvy and Mather 1992). By the end of the 1980s around a dozen such schemes had been announced.

Joint ventures and buying groups are clearly attractive to retailers. The reasons for their emergence at a particular time seem to be both defensive and offensive:

● Manufacturers had made the running in starting to think and operate internationally, especially on a European scale. Leading firms such as Procter and Gamble, Unilever, Nestlé and Mars were all well advanced in planning production and – to a lesser extent – marketing, on a pan-European basis. Many retailers felt that their previous success based on buying power was being eroded.
● Most retail multiples had had their hands full growing their domestic business, and had had ample opportunity to do so; but these growth opportunities were running out.
● The cost of green-field start-ups, and the expense and difficulties of acquisitions, meant that joint ventures offered the low-risk way of learning about new markets.

- The chance to gain further real buying muscle was very attractive. As one commentator put it: 'Synergy marketing is what the new ERA says its pan-European adventure is all about. But worried manufacturers know it better under its old name, buying power.'

So far, the main activities of the groups and alliances seem to be in joint design and sourcing of own-label products and brands. There is also no doubt a great deal being learned from shared experience.

Even with customs tariffs, there is a considerable flow of goods across boundaries. A great deal of it consists of high-value capital goods and components, and most of the rest of products not available, or not made as cheaply or as well, in the importing country. The lowering of barriers will mean that, for a manufacturer in any one country, there will be the potential of a much bigger market in which to sell his or her brands, but also the probability of greater competition from manufacturers in other countries.

In many fast-moving-consumer-goods markets, the issue of cross-border trading has not been very important. The relative cost of transporting low-ticket items has meant that most competition has come from within the country. Experience has tended to suggest that a price difference of greater than 10 per cent (depending on the product field) was needed to make importing worthwhile.

In this context, the phenomenon of parallel trading has been relatively uncommon. Parallel trading occurs when an intermediary finds it profitable to import product from another country and sell it at competitive prices against the home version. For example, in a case described by the author, an agent in Germany bought stocks of a well-known internationally available brand in the UK, and sold it to German retailers at a price which enabled them to undercut rivals' prices on the German-supplied stocks. The German subsidiary of the manufacturer complained bitterly to headquarters, demanding that they should force the UK subsidiary to increase its price. The UK company was reluctant to do so, for very good local marketing reasons.

Figure 10.3 Parallel trading

At the time of writing, then, the internationalization of retailers is beginning, if cautiously. Continental chains look enviously at UK retailers' margins, and wish to learn about information systems and own label. UK retailers gain the chance to learn about tempting new markets at low cost. There seems little doubt that joint ventures will lead to greater cooperation and in many cases to merger or acquisition. Whatever happens, buying power will increase, and will put further pressure on manufacturers, either through direct bargaining, or through parallel trading (see Figure 10.3).

With freer markets, such problems will become more common. Some people feel that already the price differential which can be sustained has fallen, and are worried about the additional complications which seem likely to arise. Since the problem is particularly relevant to Europe, it is interesting to compare the situation with the USA, which after all is not dissimilar to Europe in size and population.

In the USA, the size of the country and the regional differences mean that many markets are treated regionally. For a single brand, marketing programmes are likely to be quite different in say the North-East from the West. A manufacturer will commonly offer much better terms in a low-share region for his brand than in a high-share one, and brand shares of even very well-known brands vary considerably across the country. In this situation, intermediaries known as converters carry out what Europeans call parallel trading. Although this can be an irritation, it seems not to be a major problem for US manufacturers; they feel able to manage the situation. What it does imply is that there must at least be good communication and coordination between the regions. That is the lesson for Europeans.

The Common Market and the regulation of trade

1993, as is well known, was supposed to see the arrival of a true common market, with no trade barriers between member states. This is of course a complex matter and subject to delicate political negotiation. Similarly, GATT and other trade regulating bodies are trying to sustain the idea of free trade between all nations, against a variety of protective devices. The tides of free trade and protectionism ebb and flow, and it would be foolish to try to predict the exact situation which will prevail at any particular time and place.

In general, and with hesitation, it may be said that overt barriers to trade will decline, that customs tariffs and restrictive quotas will fall for most goods in most countries. This trend may be reversed (though it would be disastrous for most trading nations); for our purposes, it will be assumed that trade will be freer and barriers lower. What are the implications for business?

Manufacturers' response to changes

Clearly many of the changes outlined above have been in progress for some time, and some manufacturers have anticipated or reacted to them. In addition there are other forces pushing companies in new directions, in particular technology and competition.

Leading manufacturers have already become significantly more international in their strategy and organization. In many cases the move seems to have been driven mainly by the single-minded search for manufacturing efficiency. Although this does not invariably mean building fewer, larger plants and cutting out small, less efficient ones, that pattern is common. Increasingly, one plant serves several countries with a brand, even though minor variations are necessary (often to meet local legal requirements). Flexible manufacturing technology can accommodate such changes while still offering economies of scale.

Such moves are not market-driven; they are made possible by the changes in people and markets set out above. The lucky fact that people in different countries are becoming more alike allows manufacturers to make the most of production efficiencies available to them. The multinational manufacturers are tending to pour marketing resources into those markets and brands which are most susceptible to becoming international. They may be hastening processes which are happening anyway.

In becoming more international, manufacturers are also looking for greater control over their national subsidiaries. Although this can mean greater standardization, this is not essential. As mentioned, some segments of some markets are becoming homogeneous, but great differences remain in others. Typically, therefore, a manufacturer will have some fairly standardized international brands, some brands which are similar in different countries but vary in formulation, name, packaging, positioning or marketing mix, and some local brands.

In terms of dealing with retailers, what manufacturers must do above all, as was suggested above from American experience, is ensure coordination. Because of falling barriers and the increasing danger of parallel trading and multinational buyers, they must coordinate prices, trade terms, allowances and promotions across boundaries. This does not mean that these should all be the same in all countries, but that the possibility of interaction must be considered. Managers will want to optimize the balance between multinational efficiency and local closeness to the market.

In some leading companies, sales directors from around Europe meet regularly to coordinate policies and exchange information. Others are adopting more radical reorganizations and setting up whole new structures to deal with the opportunities and threats of the new Europe. Lever Europe, for example, has been set up in Brussels to manage all the national companies. Strategic direction is set at headquarters, and national marketing directors have less control over their total strategy; on the other hand, they also have lead responsibility for a European brand. Other manufacturers are adopting similar structures, or ways of ensuring European coordination.

The problem is much more severe for the medium-sized and smaller manufacturers, many of whom operate only in one domestic market or in just a few. Anyone working on a single-market level is likely to feel an extra squeeze from the international buying groups, and extra competition from international manufacturers. Once again, the very large, powerful brands and the small, niche brands will be protected; but those in the middle will be very exposed.

Like the retailers, many of these smaller manufacturers are looking to joint ventures and alliances to tackle the new problems and opportunities. Some seem to be doing very little. They all face huge and exciting challenges, which perhaps are the subject of a different book.

Summary

There is an undoubted trend towards greater internationalization in business, although arguments continue as to exactly how far it has reached. The chapter looks at developments as they affect consumers, retailers and manufacturers.

Within Europe in particular, and especially among the young, common patterns are emerging which have implications for both manufacturers and retailers. This does not mean that standardized European brands and campaigns can be introduced without thought and research.

Amongst retailers, there are common patterns, but truly international companies have been slow to develop. In the late 1980s some retailers began to expand across borders, and a surge of alliances and joint ventures showed the way forward as retailers who had until then been preoccupied with their domestic markets began to look abroad. Buying groups will begin to increase buying power again, partly as a defensive measure.

With freer markets, parallel trading will increase. The experience of a similar phenomenon in the USA (converting) suggests that manufacturers can manage the situation, although a premium will be on information and coordination.

Manufacturers have led the way in developing international strategies, structures and operations. Typically, a manufacturer will have: some fairly standardized international brands; some brands which are similar in different countries but vary in formulation, name, packaging, positioning or marketing mix; and some local brands.

In terms of dealing with retailers, what manufacturers must do above all is ensure coordination. They must coordinate prices, trade terms, allowances and promotions across boundaries.

Further reading

Kaynak, Erdener (ed) (1988), *Transnational Retailing*, Berlin: Walter de Gruyter.

Levitt, T. (1983), The globalization of markets. *Harvard Business Review*, May–June, 92–102

Macharzina, K. and Staehle, W. H. (1986), *European Approaches to International Management*, Berlin: Walter de Gruyter.

Nelson, Elizabeth (1989), Marketing in 1992 and beyond, *RSA Journal*, April.

Ogilvy and Mather (1992), *1992 – So Near and Yet so Far; The Single European Market and How to Profit from It*, London: Ogilvy and Mather.

11
The future

It is a bold, indeed foolish, writer who sets down in cold print predictions for the future. Everyone remembers the nineteenth-century expert who predicted confidently that traffic in London could not continue to grow at its then rate, because soon after 1900 Piccadilly Circus would be two feet deep in horse manure. Given the increasing rate of change, forecasting the future becomes even more hazardous.

We must still try to look ahead, however, so that we can try to prepare for what lies in store. Earlier in the book the use of scenarios was recommended. Here are two scenarios setting out what may face consumer goods manufacturers in Europe within the next ten years.

The death of brands – a worst-case scenario

In this case we shall posit certain trends in the main variables of social change – media effectiveness, retailer power, competition, other markets, and government regulation – and then assess their joint impact on manufacturers' brands.

Social change

The trends identified by many commentators accelerate. Individualism is the dominant value ('Be different from the Jones's'), leading to increasingly segmented markets. People's individualism and need to control the complexity of their lives fragments mass audiences. Shoppers become increasingly demanding, sophisticated and sceptical of advertising claims; they are unwilling to pay a large premium for a brand name when the retailer's brand is of equal quality. Brand loyalty declines; experience of product reliability and word-of-mouth become the major influences on buying decisions. Time management pressures are intensified by dual-career families and increasing desire and opportunity to pursue multiple goals; shopping becomes more of a chore.

Media effectiveness

The social changes mentioned fragment audiences: time-shifting using video-recorders, and zapping of commercials, mean that network television cannot reach mass audiences. Cable and satellite channels fragment the audiences still further. Costs continue to rise faster than inflation. The editorial standard of tabloid newspapers means that consumers do not trust advertising in them. Environmental sensitivities and road safety considerations limit the availability of poster sites. Many categories of advertising are banned in cinemas because of the age of the audience.

Retailer power

Concentration continues to grow. A small number of multinational retailers emerges in each main sector; between them, they account for 80 per cent of turnover. Their scanning data give them unrivalled market knowledge, which they are unwilling to share with manufacturers. Each expands its category coverage to counteract low-growth markets, so pressure on space is intensified.

Competition

With retailers dominating, the provision of adequate products produced to guaranteed quality specifications and delivered to a rigorous schedule becomes the norm. Japanese and other South-East Asian competitors enter European consumer-goods markets, applying their supreme manu-facturing skills learned in other markets. Competition is open within

Europe, and US competition does not grow less. Increasingly entrepreneurial attitudes are encouraged, and small manufacturers constantly spring up locally.

Government regulation

Governmental and supra-governmental legislation (EC) set strict controls on products, labelling, and advertising, while imposing extra burdens on companies in relation to packaging, pollution and other liabilities.

Other markets

Other markets – in newly industrializing countries and the Third World – do not offer any relief, since they will either produce and protect their own emerging manufacturers, or be too poor or too unstable to provide profit opportunities.

Effect on manufacturers' brands

The trends produce a vicious spiral in which major brands cannot be sustained, advertising is cut, margins come under pressure, shelf space is limited, retailers' brands increase their share, new competitors are willing to meet the retailers' demands, brand loyalty is further eroded. . . . The major manufacturers simply cannot make enough profit to reinvest in brand development and support. One by one their brands disappear from the shelves. They themselves either turn to packing for retailers, or they are taken over, or they simply die.

Note that this scenario is based on trends which already exist, and on extrapolations which are not extreme (though the conclusion may be). Everything here has been identified and commented on widely. It is a plausible hypothesis.

An optimistic scenario

The same general headings will be used to give a different picture of a possible future.

Social change

The pendulum swings back. Family life becomes the norm. Religious observance and conformity become dominant. Reaction to too much change in the past leads to a general conservatism. People seek reassurance in the known and familiar. Belief in authority figures and sources is common.

Media effectiveness

The mass audience wants what is regular and predictable; the major TV networks dominate, with a small number of additional but similar channels. The price of air time is reduced by increased competition. Mass tabloid newspapers return to respectability. All media are seen as credible sources, and advertising messages are accepted with only moderate scepticism. People seek information on products in mass media as well as from friends and family.

Retailer power

Consumer reaction against queuing and poor service limits growth of the multiples. New outlets and competitors eat into their share. Home and tele-shopping grow, providing further competition. The balance of power swings away from retailers.

Competition

The Japanese continue to be unable to crack the cultural problem, and make no inroads in mass consumer markets. Increasing national loyalties of consumers protects local manufacturers.

Government regulation

Governments refer retailers to the Monopolies Commission and their equivalent. European takeovers of other retailers are blocked by the European Commission. Stricter standards are imposed on the sale of some goods (e.g. baby foods), increasing retailers' costs. Planning permission is refused for large new retail developments.

Other markets

European manufacturers are able to use a strong and stable base to increase penetration of other markets. Their skills and world economies of scale give them a dominant advantage in NICs. Political stability and International Monetary Fund-imposed policies allow some Third World countries to offer useful markets.

Effect on manufacturers' brands

Successful manufacturers are able to consolidate their existing business base. The swing back in the balance of power gives them a reasonable margin to reinvest in brand development. New technology allows them to become more efficient.

This is not quite a turning back of the clock, although it may smack of wishful thinking in parts. Social change is not one-way, and although history does not repeat itself, it does show cyclical tendencies.

Need for more specific scenarios

The two scenarios given are of course deliberately extreme, and rather general. Manufacturers in each particular industry will need to construct their own versions, looking in detail at the forces at work in their markets. What is important is to look at the evidence objectively and construct scenarios that are actually possible, even if they are unpalatable. For example, the dominance of a few retail chains in certain markets will not disappear quickly, if ever. There is no evidence that governments are worried about retail concentration, as the retailers have so far been able to convince them that their efficiency is in the public's interest rather than the reverse.

Short of the appearance and rapid growth of some new form of competition to them, the major retail multiples will continue to be very powerful for the next few years. Rivalry between them, on the American pattern, may offer the best hope of redressing the balance towards manufacturers. Even here, however, it does not seem that the success of, say, discounters, will offer much relief to manufacturers.

What is to be done?

If the future cannot be predicted with accuracy, then certain features can be discerned. Retailer power is not going to go away, and may increase in some areas. All manufacturers must therefore organize themselves to deal with this situation.

The message of this book is essentially a simple one, and can be summed up in a few sentences. Translating the precepts into practice is more difficult, but the days of easy profits for manufacturers are over. Every manufacturer selling to consumers through retailers must check that the company has thought through the implications of the major changes that have happened and are still happening, and that it is taking appropriate action. What follows is a checklist which can be used to see where you are. Much of it is simple and obvious, but few companies can honestly say that they have done everything on the list as thoroughly as they know they should. Many have hardly started.

The first imperative is that boards must make two things absolute priorities: brands, and customer service. The building and maintenance of strong brands, preferably on an international basis, must be the highest priority, since they offer the only chance of long-term survival and success. The task is not easy, and increasing competition and retailer power will make it more and more challenging – but there is no other way.

The issue of how to serve customers better offers the opportunity to gain a real competitive advantage – or to lose ground which will be extremely difficult to make up. The aim should be to become the preferred supplier of the major multiples in your markets. Customers must become a board-level concern in a way that they have not been, and radical decisions will need to be taken as to how to re-engineer the company to deliver outstanding customer service.

Within these strategic imperatives, every company should carry out the following tasks.

- Understand your consumers – who they are, what they want, what part your brands play in their lives, how they use them, what benefits are important to them, what is missing.
- Look into the future – identify the factors that are producing change in your consumers, and predict how this will affect your markets.
- Understand your competitors – analyse the structure of your markets, and identify the forces which are driving change.

- Understand your customers – who they are, what their strategies are, where your brands fit within those strategies, what their problems and opportunities are and how you can help them.
- Build an information system – identify all the information you need to guide your strategy, help your decision making and implement and control your plans; make sure that the right information is available to the people who need it when they need it. This will include information on customers and competitors, and on international and external trends, as well as straight market data. Because of the demands of the new customer relationships, it will also include internal cost data from manufacturing and distribution, perhaps in new forms; it should include customer profitability data.
- Analyse your brand portfolio – be realistic about the future of each of your brands, given the data on consumers, customers and competitors you have gathered. Which will definitely survive as major brands, which will need a lot of remedial help, which are in danger? Check that you will generate the cash necessary to support the brands in the way they will need.
- Develop a brand strategy – decide on the actions needed over the next few years to achieve your objectives; decide on whether or not to make retailers' brands.
- Develop a customer strategy – take a stance on whether you will be a strong independent, a partner, or a responsive supplier. Target the major customer groups and accounts, deciding on a strategy for each.
- Fix clear objectives and budgets for brands and customers – decide what is needed to achieve your objectives, set budgets and allocate responsibility for decisions on spending. Make people accountable.
- Think customers – make sure that customer thinking penetrates deeply into the company, into all the departments whose activities do affect the relationship even if they are not yet aware of it.
- Rethink your organization structure – make sure that your structure helps you to deliver the information and actions needed to implement your strategies. List the tasks that relate to customers and allocate them to those best able to carry them out (not necessarily those whose job it has traditionally been).
- Build business teams – make sure that everyone who contributes to the total delivery of a brand to customers and consumers is involved. Make sure that information flows within the team so that action can be coordinated.
- Improve the quality of the people dealing with customer service – managers dealing with major retailers must be of a calibre and status equal to those in brand development.

- Implement a training programme – ensure that national account managers and others dealing with customers are fully trained in direct product profitability and space management models, and in negotiation and presentation skills. Use training to implant customer thinking and build teams.
- Review recruitment and selection policies – decide what sort of people are going to be needed not just today but in the future in your new organization. Plan to have them available and prepared. Ensure that all marketing managers have significant experience dealing with customers.

Summary

There are enormous problems in predicting the future, but businesses must do so in order to be ready for the changes ahead. The use of scenarios is recommended.

A worst-case scenario takes a pessimistic view of all the trends previously discussed.

Social change

The trends visible today accelerate. Individualism is the dominant value. Shoppers become increasingly demanding, sophisticated and sceptical of advertising claims and brands. Brand loyalty declines; shopping becomes more of a chore.

Media effectiveness

The social changes mentioned fragment audiences. Costs continue to rise faster than inflation.

Retailer power

Concentration continues to grow. A small number of multinational retailers emerges in each main sector; between them, they account for 80 per cent of turnover.

Competition

Japanese and other South-East Asian competitors enter European consumer-goods markets, applying their supreme manufacturing skills learned in other markets.

Government regulation

Governmental and supra-governmental legislation (EC) set strict controls on products, labelling and advertising, while imposing extra burdens on companies in relation to pollution and other liabilities.

Other markets

Other markets – in newly industrializing countries and the Third World – do not offer any relief.

Effect on manufacturers' brands

The trends produce a vicious spiral in which major brands cannot be sustained, advertising is cut, margins come under pressure, shelf space is limited, retailers' brands increase their share, new competitors are willing to meet the retailers' demands, brand loyalty is further eroded. . . .

The major manufacturers simply cannot make enough profit to reinvest in brand development and support. One by one their brands disappear from the shelves. They themselves either turn to packing for retailers, or they are taken over, or they simply die.

An optimistic scenario based on similar factors would see manufacturers able to consolidate their present position. Each company needs to produce its own, much more specific, scenarios, including best- and worst-case views.

Whatever the view, retailer power is here to stay, at least in the foreseeable future. Manufacturers must make strong brands and customer service their priorities at board level. They should go through a checklist of actions to ensure that they are doing all they can to meet the challenges and make the most of opportunities offered:

- Understand your consumers.
- Look into the future.

- Understand your competitors.
- Understand your customers.
- Build an information system.
- Analyse your brand portfolio.
- Develop a brand strategy.
- Develop a customer strategy.
- Fix clear objectives and budgets for brands and customers.
- Think customers.
- Rethink your organization structure.
- Build business teams.
- Improve the quality of people dealing with customers.
- Implement a training programme.
- Review recruitment and selection policies.

Appendix 1
Retailers' brands

Many of the examples in this appendix are taken from a Management Horizons publication of 1986.

Store name brands

Most grocery brands fall into this category. Examples are Sainsbury in the UK, Kroger in the USA, Aldi in Germany and Albert Heijn in Holland. In other markets, there are Next and Habitat in the UK, L. L. Bean in the USA, Hennes in Sweden and elsewhere.

Retailer-controlled name brands

The best-known example is of course Marks and Spencers' St Michael name, which is more or less synonymous with its owner. Dixons in the UK has its own Miranda brand for photographic goods and Saisho for audio and video products. Foto Quelle in Germany uses Revue for cameras and Apollo for spectacles.

Designer labels

These are not confined to manufacturers, but have been adopted by some retailers as well. The Limited chain in the USA launched a collection by

Kenzo, while Sears Roebuck carries the Diane von Furstenburg Style for Living range of home fashion products.

Licensed names

A similar tactic is the identification of a range with a famous personality (real or imaginary), but exclusive to one retailer. Examples are Winnie the Pooh, Evonne Goolagong, and Cheryl Tiegs ranges sold by Sears Roebuck.

Generics

These are absolutely basic products, usualy limited to a few commodity fields such as sugar, packaged in very plain style and sold at a rock-bottom price. Introduced originally in France by the Carrefour chain, generics were adopted by most supermarket multiples. By 1980 most had dropped them again, as they appeared to have outlived their usefulness, but forms of generic have reappeared, often as specialist help-yourself stores or departments (e.g. Weigh and Save in the UK). Generics have also appeared in fields outside grocery, such as stationery.

Appendix 2
Porter's elements of industry structure

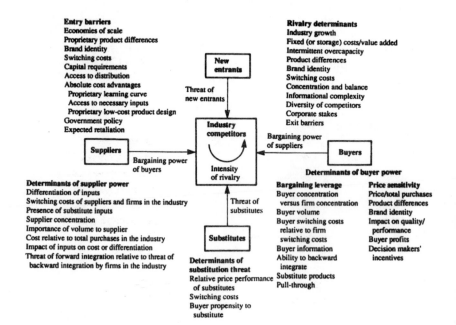

Entry barriers
Economies of scale
Proprietary product differences
Brand identity
Switching costs
Capital requirements
Access to distribution
Absolute cost advantages
  Proprietary learning curve
  Access to necessary inputs
  Proprietary low-cost product design
Government policy
Expected retaliation

Rivalry determinants
Industry growth
Fixed (or storage) costs/value added
Intermittent overcapacity
Product differences
Brand identity
Switching costs
Concentration and balance
Informational complexity
Diversity of competitors
Corporate stakes
Exit barriers

Threat of new entrants

Bargaining power of suppliers

Determinants of supplier power
Differentiation of inputs
Switching costs of suppliers and firms in the industry
Presence of substitute inputs
Supplier concentration
Importance of volume to supplier
Cost relative to total purchases in the industry
Impact of inputs on cost or differentiation
Threat of forward integration relative to threat of
  backward integration by firms in the industry

Determinants of buyer power

Bargaining leverage
Buyer concentration
  versus firm concentration
Buyer volume
Buyer switching costs
  relative to firm
  switching costs
Buyer information
Ability to backward
  integrate
Substitute products
Pull-through

Price sensitivity
Price/total purchases
Product differences
Brand identity
Impact on quality/
  performance
Buyer profits
Decision makers'
  incentives

Threat of substitutes

Determinants of substitution threat
Relative price performance
  of substitutes
Switching costs
Buyer propensity to
substitute

Source: Porter, Michael E. (1985), *Competitive Advantage*, The Free Press.

Index